RENEWALS 458-45
DATE DUE

**WITHDRAWN
UTSA LIBRARIES**

Travel Narratives in Dialogue

Currents in Comparative Romance Languages and Literatures

Tamara Alvarez-Detrell and Michael G. Paulson
General Editors

Vol. 155

PETER LANG
New York • Washington, D.C./Baltimore • Bern
Frankfurt am Main • Berlin • Brussels • Vienna • Oxford

Shannon Marie Butler

Travel Narratives in Dialogue

Contesting Representations of Nineteenth-Century Peru

PETER LANG
New York • Washington, D.C./Baltimore • Bern
Frankfurt am Main • Berlin • Brussels • Vienna • Oxford

Library of Congress Cataloging-in-Publication Data

Butler, Shannon Marie.
Travel narratives in dialogue: contesting representations
of nineteenth-century Peru / Shannon Marie Butler.
p. cm. — (Currents in comparative Romance languages and literatures; vol. 155)
Includes bibliographical references.
1. Travel writing—Peru. 2. Peru—Description and travel.
I. Title. II. Series.
G151.B887   918.504'5—dc22   2008003347
ISBN 978-0-8204-9520-0
ISSN 0893-5963

Bibliographic information published by **Die Deutsche Bibliothek**.
Die Deutsche Bibliothek lists this publication in the "Deutsche
Nationalbibliografie"; detailed bibliographic data is available
on the Internet at http://dnb.ddb.de/.

The paper in this book meets the guidelines for permanence and durability
of the Committee on Production Guidelines for Book Longevity
of the Council of Library Resources.

© 2008 Peter Lang Publishing, Inc., New York
29 Broadway, 18th floor, New York, NY 10006
www.peterlang.com

All rights reserved.
Reprint or reproduction, even partially, in all forms such as microfilm,
xerography, microfiche, microcard, and offset strictly prohibited.
Printed in Germany

Dedicated to Milagros Lagos and José Guaman Chicaiza
and to my grandfather, Lea Abbott

Contents

Acknowledgments ix

Chapter One. Introduction 1

Chapter Two. Ghosts in the Machine: Citational Practices,
  Travel and Ideological Itineraries 21

Chapter Three. Constructing Peru: Imperialist Representations
  of a "Backward" Nation 53

Chapter Four. Talking Back to Center(s) 81

Chapter Five. Conclusion 115

Bibliography 119

Acknowledgments

I wish to thank my former adviser, Dr. Fernando Unzueta, for his tireless support of my research and for his constant encouragement of my work throughout my graduate studies career at The Ohio State University and beyond. I also thank those who offered their expertise and helped me to revise this work: Dr. Maureen Ahern and Dr. Abril Trigo-Ehlers. I am especially grateful to Dr. Ahern for suggesting that I study at the Centro Bartolomé de Las Casas in Cuzco, Peru and for recommending me to their program. Finally, I am very grateful for the patience and understanding of two people who supported me through the duration of this process: Dean Huston and Ron Houchin.

• CHAPTER ONE •

Introduction

> *Ahora mismo se publica en París una obra sobre viajes que si se juzga de la verdad de las noticias referentes a varios pueblos del mundo, por las de las que tocan al Perú, puede decirse que sus autores pretenden escribir una novela cuyos personajes tengan todos el tipo grosero del salvaje.*
>
> Manuel A. Fuentes,
> Lima: Apuntes históricos, descriptivos, estadísticos y de costumbres (1867)

> If one were to judge a travel book, recently published in Paris, according to its veracity in regards to the various places around the world and regarding Peru itself, one could say that its authors pretend to write a novel whose characters have all the crude mannerisms of a savage.
>
> (Translation mine)

The study of nineteenth-century travel literature has garnered an intense amount of attention among scholars in recent years. One might ask, however, what makes travel writing from the 1800s particularly intriguing?

More so than in centuries prior to the 1800s, the genre exploded in many ways. First of all, the discursive modes with which to narrate a travel text expanded during the period. In looking at European travelers who ventured to Latin America during the eighteenth century, a travel writer was more likely than not commissioned by the state to contribute to what Mary Louise Pratt considers the global "planetary consciousness" through international scientific expeditions (Pratt 15). The discursive mode for constructing and narrating one's findings was largely scientific in tone in which the "voice of the scientist predominates, structuring the discourse around measurements, climatic phenomena, and so forth" (18). This type of discursive mode was largely statistical and "virtually devoid of anecdote" (20).

However, with the rise of Romanticism's emphasis on the individual, travel writers by the 1820s no longer had to solely employ scientific modes of narration in their texts, but rather they could supplement the scientific with the "spiritual esthetics of Romanticism" (121). At this point in time, anecdotal evidence could be incorporated into the text as well as personal information and commentary. The search for narrating the invisible forces in the world and looking for essences within what was observed was also permitted entry in the travel narrative by this point (121).

This new flexibility of narrating one's journey occurred in the very century that Paul Fussell terms "the Bourgeois Age" in Europe (Fussell 271). At this time in European travel literature, the genre became legitimated as a literary genre (273). The popularity, publication and consumption of travel narratives exploded especially toward the mid 1800s and throughout the century. Travel abroad became more feasible during this period with the advent of iron vessels or steam ships along side the economic prosperity of the middle and upper-middle classes (273). More people could afford better education, travel abroad, and the purchase of books. As a result, the book-publishing market in Europe exploded (Ramos 80; Fussell 274). Readerships now included both men and women and book publishers were open to accepting travelogues written by what Pascal Riviale refers to as "informal" travelers—those travelers who venture to other lands not as commissioned officials or scientists but as amateur and adventurous travelers (Riviale 277). Both general and intellectual readerships produced such a demand that women travel writers entered the genre, and they were often successful at it.

These European readers and U.S. American readers were not the only readers interested in the histories, travel guides and travel texts written by their compatriots. In the case of such works that involved the representation of nineteenth-century Peru, texts written about Peru by non-Peruvians were also read by Peruvian intellectuals of the period as both Mark Thurner and Jorge Cañizares-Esguerra point out. Whereas Cañizares-Esguerra notes that travel accounts written about Peru were consumed by Peruvian intellectuals, Thurner finds that histories about Peru were also read by Peruvians (Thurner, "Peruvian Genealogies" 163; Cañizares-Esguerra 91). One would be remiss to think that, in the case of Peru, Peruvian-written guidebooks, travel texts and histories didn't reach an audience in Western European countries and in the United States (Ramos 80). For example, during the course of my research, I have found that many of the imperialist travel writers included in the corpus of travelogues I've examined for the purposes of this book refer to and cite works authored by Peruvians during the nineteenth century, such as José Hipolito Unanúe's *Observaciones sobre el clima de Lima* (1815) as well as his *Nuevo día del Perú* (1824); Manuel A. Fuentes' *Lima: Apuntes históricos, descriptivos, estadísticos y costumbres* (1865); Mariano Felipe Paz Soldán's *Historia del Perú independiente* (1868); and Juan Bustamante's *Viaje al Antiguo Mundo* (1849).

As pertains to the diversity of travel-writing subjects that enter the arena, not only were women engaging in the genre, but so, too, were Latin American writers—in this case, Peruvian writers. This is an important point to underscore. Often there occurs the monolithic binary of center and periphery (or margin) in the imperial context, in which it is assumed that those who represent the periphery are without agency due to the control of centers. Perhaps Peruvian writers' works would fall upon deaf ears, so-to-speak, out of the reception of imperial centers. Sometimes, though, they were heard.

This underscores how delving into the texts of nineteenth-century travelers (whether from the U.S., Europe or Peru) offers the post-colonialist researcher a wealth of possibility indestabilizing Eurocentric or U.S. American imperialist ideologies. Since the post-colonialist is often eager to expose contestatory voices to imperialist agendas, this period and genre offers an opportunity to unearth such voices. In the case of Peruvian travel writers, they implicitly and sometimes explicitly challenged the representations of Peruvian culture proffered by imperialist travelers to Peru. I do not want to suggest that there was an equal opportunity for circulating contestatory, Peruvian-authored representations to adequately silence those written by imperialist writers whose numbers were higher in circulation and inundating the imperialist readership and imaginary.

The immense circulation of travel texts which repeated the "dismal portraits" that Cañizares-Esguerra finds in the British and French travel writing about the Spanish American colonies, and that I find in European and U.S. American travel texts about Peru throughout the nineteenth century, perpetuated the idea of a supposed inferiority of Latin American peoples and nations (Cañizares-Esguerra 91).

The messages found in such narratives carried and supported an imperialist ethos of cultural, moral and political superiority over such peoples. This is where the power dynamics involved with representation in travel discourse becomes an important issue for those researchers who examine literary texts from a discursive and cultural framework.

Postcolonialist theorists and critics such as Mary Louise Pratt, David Spurr, A.E. Metawlli and Alison Blunt examine how travel writing, like any form of writing, constitutes a political act, since "travel writing rejoined the expansion of knowledge of the natural world with the expansion of the capitalist world system, previously seen as ideologically split, which suggests attempts to impose order and the interdependence of power, 'truth,' and knowledge within imperial discourse" (Blunt 33).[1] In other words, European and American travel writing linked itself with and sustained imperialist logic.

Travel writing helped to support European and U.S. imperialist agendas (whether explicitly or implicitly) by reinforcing the imperialist world-views of their home countries. The travelers' home countries represented the paragon of civilization and, thus, put the writing travelers in a position of supposed superiority over other lands. The travel writing subject gains a position of authority through all he/she sees, classifies and explains regarding an other culture, while his/her seemingly objective mode of discourse is filtered through an imperialist world-view. Travel writing was heavily influenced by the scientific discourses of the period, which incorporated taxonomic modes of representation; it was also affected by racial sciences of the period such as physiognomy and phrenology. Both of these influences induced writing-subjects to classify all the types of "others" found in post-colonies whose inhabitants lived in a miscegenated world. Such classificatory surveillance is done seemingly from a passive (and, therefore, presumably innocent) vantage point that ultimately possesses in the name (explicitly or implicitly) of the traveler's own culture. The writing subject borrows the discourses of his/her world-view. Such as those of racial and moral superiority based on "paradigms of progress and development" (Pratt 74). These discourses in turn naturalize the traveler's presence and authority as well as that of the empire he/she represents. For this reason, travel texts cannot be viewed as isolated from the ideological and political/economic contexts that surround them.

Colonialism/Post-colonialism

A post-colonialist critique of colonization, imperialism and neo-colonialism is in order before considering how travel texts were connected and helped in disseminating certain imperialist designs.

In *Colonialism/Postcolonialism*, Ania Loomba deconstructs a definition of colonization found in the *Oxford English Dictionary* that evacuates any sense of power and the rigid hierarchies produced by an empire's power that put in place an unequal relationship between the colonizers and the colonized. What she finds to be a dangerous, or at best, misguided definition of "colonization" follows:

> A settlement in a new country...a body of people who settle in a new locality, forming a community subject to or connected with their parent state; the community so formed, consisting of the original settlers and their descendents and successors, as long as the connection with the parent state is kept up. (1)

The problem that arises from such a definition is that it "avoids any reference to people other than the colonizers." The inhabitants become invisible as if they were never there before colonizers arrived. Thus, "it evacuates the word 'colonialism' of any implication of an encounter between peoples, or of conquest and domination" (1-2). A key component the definition fails to note is that, besides the military and administrative power involved in conquest, there is an economic dominance that is crucial to colonialism. Loomba points out that it is important to consider that "in whichever direction human beings and materials traveled [during the process of colonization], the profits always flowed back into the so-called 'mother country,'" rendering colonies in a captive economic state and privileging "markets for European goods" and consumption (3-4). Loomba continues: "The essential point is that although European colonialisms involved a variety of techniques and patterns of domination...all of them produced the economic imbalance that was necessary for the growth of European capitalism and industry" (4). As we will find in the texts written by imperialist travel writers, they offer examples of perpetuating the desire of a particular mode of Progress, which aligned itself with the overarching imperialist desire of dominating a "global system" of capitalism (6).

In addition, the definition admittedly constrained by the demands of a dictionary's format of condensed entries also erases a point of continuance often found in post-colonies once they've broken off from their parent countries. The definition suggests that once the relationship is split off, dominance and control of the former parent country is terminated. However, Loomba underscores the point that systems of unequal economic relations set in place by colonialism often contined even after the split. Herein lies the importance of the term, *imperialism*, and a deconstruction of it, since it is often used synonymously with *colonialism*. The economic lines drawn during colonialisms supported an imperialist "global system" of capitalism. However, imperialist capitalism supported by colonialism does not merely end in a colony's independence. Loomba is clear on this point: if imperialism is defined as a political system in which an imperial centre governs colonised countries, then the granting of political independence signals the end of empire, the collapse of imperialism. However, if imperialism is primarily an economic system of penetration and control of markets, then political changes do not basically affect it, and may even redefine the term as in a case of 'American imperialism,' which wields enormous military and economic power across the globe without direct political control (6).

An indirect form of political control exists in the circulation and reproduction of imperialist discourse. This pertains to what critics such as Bill Ashcroft, Gareth Griffiths and Helen Tiffin deem to be *informal imperialism*, a form of imperialism which functions through a "continuous development of imperial rhetoric and of imperial representation of the rest of the globe"

(Ashcroft, *Key Concepts*, 126). Such rhetoric and representation posits and perpetuates "a belief in European [or U.S. American] cultural dominance—a belief in a superior right to exploit the world's resources" (125).

Who, among others, help fortify and disseminate this belief? In addition to "explorers, missionaries, fortune hunters and settlers" from imperialist nations who travel to *other* lands, one finds the "ordinary travelers" (124). Pascal Riviale stresses that, no matter whether or not a traveler during this period was consciously contributing to imperialist designs, the fundamental desire for the foreign travelers (to Peru, in this case) was to achieve the following: "aprender la humanidad en su globalidad, cuantificar su diversidad, y finalmente explicar...los mecanismos...(según se pensaba) que habían conducido a ciertas naciones a un estado de desarrollo, a un nivel de civilización juzgado infinitamente más elevado que el de otras" (Riviale 348).

For this reason, I opt to term the European and U.S. American travelers as "imperialist" travel writers because they embue their representations of Peruvian *others* with what Antoinette Burton calls an "imperialist ethos" (Burton 138). In other words, writers such as J.J. von Tschudi, Madeleine Dahlgren and Flora Tristan produce representations of Peruvian cultures through a belief in their own superiority over the Peruvians they represent whether on moral, cultural and/or racial grounds (138). They are purveyors of imperialist discourse who contribute to another form of power—neither militaristic nor economic—that helped confirm "the hegemony of imperialism" throughout the nineteenth century (Ashcroft, *Key Concepts* 127).

Prevailing Trends in Travel Studies
Several trends appear in the scholarship with respect to imperialist travel narrative during the nineteenth century. First, most scholars point their attention primarily to the colonial sites of Africa and Asia. Secondly, often such studies either tend to view the imperialist subject as completely in control of the Knowledge/Power or simply do not include discussions of the master subject's vulnerability. However, these two tendencies ignore, first of all, that Latin America was also a site of imperialist designs during the same period and, secondly, that writing subjects from various empires to Latin America often depended upon the local knowledges that its inhabitants possessed. These local knowledges helped both to guide the traveler's itinerary of formidable sites and sights and to authenticate the truth value of his/her travelogue. These two points are important because they begin to de-center the notion of a "master subject." The idea of a master subject solidified during the European Romantic period that subscribes to the notion that the Subject was in control of the truth he/she revealed as author. Michael Foucault, however,

critiqued such notion of the author-subject and preferred "to call the author the 'author-function'" (Mills 37). This is not to say that the author-function is over-determined by social forces and discourses before the pen strikes the paper. Rather the author-function is a term used to show how the author is "not a coherent entity" but a conglomerate of how the author-function's own desire for expression is additionally "mediated by, discourse, i.e., the writing system and its cultural rules" (Mills 7).

One scholar in particular, Mary Louise Pratt, has brought Latin America to the forefront of postcolonial studies concerning imperialist travel writing.[2] Other scholars have followed in her stead such as Staton Catlin, Deborah Poole, June Hahner, Fernando Coronil, Antonio Barrera-Osorio, Jorge Cañizares-Esguerra, and Ricardo Salvatore. Pratt has also brought attention to the problematic nature of the supposed master subject in travel-narrative. In her *Imperial Eyes*, Pratt questions the boundaries of center and periphery by examining the transculturating processes that take place within the gathering of knowledge about the "other" via the European, nineteenth-century travel narrative regarding South American nations. This need for gleaning information from local sources and informants undercuts the monolithic notion of a totalizing authority on the part of the master subject and imperialist control.

Although Pratt does highlight the participatory nature (whether through a mode of support or resistance) of those viewed as "other," most of that participation according to her chosen corpus of travel texts remains bound within the covers of European travel texts. Pratt admits that her book "leaves both Europe *and travel literature* behind to examine instances of non-European expression developed in interaction with European repertoires" (5; my emphasis). In other words, when Pratt focuses on South American texts, she sidesteps the genre of travel narrative altogether. This is a curious departure, resulting in a missed opportunity to explore what the genre of travel writing itself offers during the post-independence period: direct contestation of European representations of Latin American culture in the travel texts written by Latin Americans themselves. Those scholars who do examine travelogues written by Latin Americans choose for their corpus those narratives that involve Latin Americans' travels abroad to Europe and/or the U.S. This is the case, for example, with the studies published by David Viñas and Jacinto Rafael Fombona Iribarren.

Another tendency in this field of study is that many scholars concentrate their investigations on only one particular group of travel writers. Some academics focus solely on the imperialist writers; others concentrate only on the travel writings of women from imperialist nations; even fewer scholars consider the existence of travelogues written by Latin Americans themselves. This trend minimizes two important issues: the intense dialogic nature of travel writing and the malleability of rhetorical tropes used in this genre as played out by different types of travel writers during this period.

Questions Raised

The idea for this study grew from a convergence of personal, creative and academic goals. During my undergraduate studies, I had the opportunity to strike up a lasting and endearing friendship with a Peruvian immigrant to the U.S., Milagros Lagos. We were able to speak candidly about our cultural differences as two women born continents apart. I was unable to go with her to Peru to visit her family when she first invited me in 1992. However, her suggestion to see Peru, as well as her friendship, led me to major in Spanish and to plan on seeing Peru some day.

While working toward my Master's degree in Spanish and Latin American Literature at The Ohio Statue University, I found that I was most attracted to Peruvian texts: especially Inca Garcilaso's *Comentarios reales*, Ricardo Palma's *Tradiciones peruanas,* and Clorinda Matto de Turner's *Aves sin nido*. Though I had already studied in Latin America before, I still had not fulfilled Milagros' goal (and mine, too) until finally in 1996, I had my chance to study Quechua and Peruvian texts in Cuzco, Peru at the Centro Bartolomé de Las Casas, visiting en route Milagros' family in Lima. My own "travel guides" for the trip were José María Arguedas' *Los ríos profundos*; *Peruvian Pageant* written by Blair Niles, a prolific woman travel-writer and novelist during the early 1900s; Pratt's *Imperial Eyes*; and *Under Tropic Skies*, an unpublished copy of a travelogue my own great-grandfather, N.C. Abbott, had written during the years 1901–1903.

In his *Under Tropic Skies*, my great-grandfather recounted his travels and missionary work in the Philippines in 1901, just three years after the U.S. waged its first battle of the Spanish-American War (which took place in the Philippine Islands). I read it on the plane flight to Peru. In his representations of Philippine culture, my great-grandfather had employed all the imperialist rhetorical tricks that I had read about in *Imperial Eyes*—a realization that weighed heavy on me. Blair Niles' narrative, though to a lesser degree, did much the same. At that point, I realized that I would embark on an academic journey to better understand the power dynamics involved in representing one's own country and that of the Other as they pertained to Peru.

Thanks to the efforts of Estuardo Nuñez to make travel texts that related to nineteenth-century Peru more accessible to scholars interested in the field, the idea for this book further evolved from reading the texts included in

Nuñez's anthologies, especially those in his *Viajeros hispanoamericanos*. David Viñas also examined Latin American travel writers, yet neither of these works provided mention of travel texts produced by nineteenth-century Peruvian nationalists. This curious absence spurred me to conduct a search through various databases under the category of "viajeros peruanos." One of the Peruvian writers who came up from this search was J. M. Valdéz y Palacios, who had written *Viaje del Cuzco a Belén en el Gran Pará*. Nuñez had edited an easily-accessible copy of the original manuscript.

Then, considering the current scholarship on nineteenth-century travel writing as it pertained to Peru, I found myself formulating questions regarding the field: why didn't studies include regional travel texts written by Latin Americans of the same period which could possibly show their direct engagement with European and North American representations of Latin America? If the object is to look at exchange, dialogue and negotiation that takes place between travelers representative of global "centers" (Europe and United States) and inhabitants of a "periphery" (Latin America), wouldn't it be useful to look at that dialogue within the genre itself, as it is played out among representative travelers from all sides? Was anybody analyzing Peruvian regional travel texts and their connection with their European and North American counterparts? Did European and North American travelers ever cite travel texts produced by Latin Americans about themselves? In other words, was the dialogue, indeed, bi-directional and not only at an "informal" level (that of orally provided information) but even at the level of written travel texts?

I set out to find answers to those basic questions, confining myself to travel texts about Peru approximately from the 1820s to the 1860s. Though I have limited the core of my corpus to six travelogues, I will also be consulting an additional set of travelogues. These supplementary texts will be consulted, especially in chapter one, in an attempt to better define the characteristics and conventions of travel literature about Peru.[3] The supplementary texts chosen are frequently cited in the travelogues that constitute the core corpus on which I concentrate much of my textual and cultural analyses.

The Corpus of Travelogues

What I consider to be my core texts for chapters one through three of this study concern certain groupings of writers, each of which represents either imperialist or Peruvian nationalist travel writers. These groupings in no way preclude me from examining the certain degree of overlapping that occurs in terms of rhetorical strategies used by all of the writers involved. In other words, to a certain degree, all of the texts will be considered in conjunction with one another in order to determine conventions concerning nineteenth-century Peru.

One of the groupings concerns men and women from global "centers" (Europe and the U.S.) who write with an *imperialist ethos* upon representing Peru and its inhabitants. According to Antoinette Burton, this ethos involves a sense of racial and/or moral superiority in light of the "other" culture (Burton 138). This grouping primarily involves the following travel narratives: J.J. von Tschudi's *Travels in Peru, during the Years 1838-1842* (1844); Flora Tristan's *Peregrinaciones de una paria* (1838); and M.V. Dahlgren's *South Sea Sketches: A Narrative* (1881).[4] Although the last text mentioned would seem to be outside of the previously stated period under consideration, it recounts Dahlgren's travels which took place in the early 1860s.

Close attention is paid to the use of *prescribed itineraries* and what I term, *ideological intineraries* common to this first grouping of writers. Mary Schriber uses the term "prescribed itineraries" to refer to the nineteenth-century traveler's allegiance to follow itineraries elaborated in predecessor texts or travelogues written about the same *other* land that they planned to travel through themselves (16-17). Upon reading the various travelogues written about nineteenth-century Peru by travelers from Western Europe and the U.S., one notes an uncanny repetition of sites (certain ruins from the pre-Inca and Inca periods as well as governmental, cultural and religious structures built during the period of Spanish colonialism) and sights (public "spectacles" and customs) that the travelers included in their narratives. This proclivity toward viewing the same or similar sites and sights written about by travelers prior to those texts which comprise the corpus of travelogues analyzed in this work exemplify Schrieber's use of the term, *prescribed itineraries*. However, I expand Schriber's term, opting instead for the term, *prescribed travel itineraries* in order to offset the term from another form of itineraries I've coined as *ideological itineraries*, which will be discussed later in this chapter.

Though the corpus of texts was chosen somewhat randomly (with the exception that they be written about Peru and published within the time frame of the 1800s), the sites and sights the travelers chose to include seem anything but random. By examining the travelers' citational practices the impact of predecessor texts becomes apparent as to the prescribed itineraries they followed, since travelers invoked predecessor texts in an effort to boost their own authority on the subject of Peru.

Regarding the travelogues examined for this study (with the exceptions of those written by Alexander von Humboldt, Flora Tristan, E. de Sartiges, and Charles Darwin), most of them were written and published during the height of Peru's Guano Age, spanning the period of the 1840s to the late 1880s.

Since travelers invoked predecessor texts in an effort to boost their own authority on the subject of Peru, by examining the travelers' citational practices, the impact of predecessor texts becomes apparent as to the prescribed travel itineraries they followed. Among those texts invoked by the travelers are Spanish (and *mestizo*, as in the case of Inca Garcilaso de la Vega) chronicles about the conquest of Peru. For example, among others, the two most frequently mentioned are Inca Garcilaso's *Comentarios reales* (1609) and Pedro Cieza de León's *La crónica del Perú* (1553). Those travelers who didn't embark on their own journeys through Peru prior to 1840, alluded to or mentioned works written during the European Romantic Period. For example, Jean-Frrançois Marmontel's *Les incas* (1777), William H. Prescott's *History of the Conquest of Peru* (1843), Alexander von Humboldt's *Views of Nature* (1808) and *Views of the Cordilleras* (1810), and W.B. Stevenson's *Residence in South America* (1825) are commonly invoked.

The basic sites (the nodal points on the itineraries) included are the famed Ciudad de los Reyes (Lima) for viewing both Andean and Spanish structures alike; Cuzco; and various Inca ruins and roadways surrounding those areas. To a lesser degree, other must-see cities included are Arequipa and Puno. As for the prescribed sights, these included what were viewed by the travelers as spectacles: bullfights, cockfights, religious processions and celebrations—all of which allowed viewing the miscegenated population in the same, shared public space, and to catch sight of the famous *tapadas*.

Schriber writes that the pressure to build one's itinerary based on predecessor texts create "blind spots" in a travel-writing subject's field of vision to the extent that travelers "undertake to find the congruence of a sight with the idea of it, with a type that derives from earlier travelers" (65). However, since the imperialist agenda requires a rhetorical ploy to legitimate its expansionist desire and since the traveler's under study explicitly suggest how their home countries could reap wealth from the natural resources Peru had to offer, I coin the term, *ideological itineraries*. The use of this coined term is offered to highlight the power dynamic involved in representing Peru and its inhabitants as a *backward* nation possessed of an *inherently inferior* national character (*known* for its *indolence* and *superstition*). The sites and sights included as part of a conventional itinerary were represented in a way to convey this supposed inferior national character, which in turn helped to sustain an ideology of *legitimate* imperialism.

The second grouping of texts involves regional travel texts produced by Peruvians, themselves. Special attention will be given to how their particular loci of enunciation makes the writers both complicit with and contestatory of imperialist discourses based on the trope of "othering". Examining the locus of enunciation involves looking at all the filtering processes that occur during the *way of saying* that results in the end product: a statement. Walter Mignolo defines the locus of enunciation as "the place (physical as well as theoretical) from which a given statement...is being pronounced" where the "desires, the interests, the alliances, and, briefly, the politics of intellectual inquiry" are located in a statement (324). A statement is not produced one-dimensionally. Examining the locus of enunciation of every statement uttered by the writing subject allows analyzing not only the disciplinary discursive forces (the scholarly allegiances through which a writing subject speaks) but also exploring the nondisciplinary forces (a writing subject's gender, class, race, nation) that affect every utterance (Mignolo 5). Pluralizing the term, *locus* to *loci*, alerts one to follow the reconfigurations of these forces that occur within the aggregate.

The need to represent Peru as a country with its own national history provided the impetus for these Peruvian travel writers to appropriate the rhetorical techniques of imperialist discourse, refashioning them into instruments with which to talk back to imperial centers. The multiple positionings (or discursive loci) that the Peruvian travel writers manage involve trying to represent Peru as a modern nation while at the same time representing the nation with a distinctive national character. The selection of texts of this grouping are: J. M. Valdéz y Palacios' *Viaje del Cuzco a Belén en el Gran Pará* (1844); Juan Bustamante's *Viaje al Antiguo Mundo* (1849); and M. A. Fuentes' *Lima: Apuntes históricos, descriptivos, estadísticos y de costumbres* (1867).

The Allure of "Investment" in Peru during the Age of Guano

> *These islands [the Chinca islands] have of late years become celebrated on account of the great quantity of guano that has been exported from them...Much has recently been written on the employment and utility of guano...The price [of a bushel of colored guano has recently undergone many fluctuations, in consequence of the great exports to Europe...Generally speaking, the interior of the country [of Peru] is well suited to all the fruits and grain of central Europe; and doubtless many of our forest trees would flourish on those Peruvian hills which now present traces of vegetation.*
>
> J.J. von Tshudi, *Travels in Peru* (1847)

The travelogues mentioned earlier were within the context of Peru's early post-independence period during the 1820s through the 1860s. At mid-century, Peru was experiencing its integration into the world economy through its heightened exports of guano. What historians call the Age of Guano marks a time in which European investment and exploitation (not without the help of a certain profiteering sector of an over-accommodating Peruvian elite) of Peru's resource of guano was rampant. In the nineteenth-century—a time during which Europe found its agricultural yields jeopardized by massive soil depletion—the discovery of guano (the excrement of marine birds) as a rich fertilizer for crops catapulted a surge of European interest in Peru's guano reserves. At the same time, many travelers were emphasizing Peru's fertile soil as a future resource for European crops. Travelers, such as von Tschudi, propose the idea of planting non-Peruvian crops and encouraging the cultivation of traditional European foodstuffs for exportation to Europe under the guise of "free" trade agreements often favoring European markets (along with a small Peruvian elite class and the various government officials during the period). It is during this period that a debate of national discourses ensued between the nation's liberal and conservative elites.[5] The Age of Guano encouraged a push for free trade measures by liberal Peruvian nationals (Gootenberg 11; Thurner 44; Clayton 123; Larson 3).

An examination of regional Peruvian travelogues during this period reveals the contest that took place for national dominance between nationalist conservatives and liberals. Such an examination exposes not only the "imagined" constructed nature of national communities, but also the different ways in which the same nation can be imagined (Anderson 7). It is within this context that we can detect the urgency with which the Peruvians talked back to imperialist and nationalist centers alike.

The travel texts gathered here exhibit the principle of what Bakhtin terms dialogism, how an utterance or discourse is embodied by a socio-historical context, by previous discourses and by the anticipation of subsequent discourses (*Dialogic* 58-59). Therefore, in order to analyze this concept, I intend to put these travel texts in dialogue with one another. Such a move is by no means artificial, since the travel writers here are all implicitly in dialogue with one another, and often times explicitly so. Some of the travel writers in this corpus, in fact, cite one another's travelogues. I propose that all of the writing subjects participating in this dialogue evidence an instability of subjectivities due to their need to engage in a constant process of establishing hierarchies; these hierarchies, in turn, are necessary to maintain their authority within imperialist, nationalist or even proto-feminist projects.[6]

In response to the questions evoked from reading the current scholarship on nineteenth-century travel writing concerning Peru, it is hoped that this study should put to rest any doubts whether or not a bidirectional dialogue took place among travel writers both Peruvian and European or from the United States within the genre itself of travel narrative. Indeed, Peruvian regional travel narratives do exist during this period. They do talk back to European and North American representations of Peru and its inhabitants. Moreover, Peruvian travel texts were frequently consulted and cited by many prominent European and United States travelers.

Chapter Descriptions
Divided into three basic chapters besides those of the introduction and conclusion, this book will discuss how nineteenth-century travel narratives share certain conventions and constitute a political act; how that political act is socially accented according to each travel writer's loci of enunciation; how Peruvian regional travelogues talk back to imperial and even *limeño* centers; and, finally, how one should not assume that the master subject is in total control of his/her discourse.

Chapter 2: Ghosts in the Machine: Citational Practices, Travel and Ideological Itineraries
Ghosts in the Machine highlights the various tropes that prevail in travel discourse during the period under consideration (early to mid 1800's) and their link with ethnography, archeology and other scientific discourses. I discuss the rhetorical strategies that travelers during this period generally employ. These involve, among others, certain geographic, social and moral itineraries, all of which intersect one another, allowing the traveler to formulate a variety of maps: geographical, temporal, and moral. In the case of geographic itineraries shared by almost all of the writers under study, there seems to be a conventional course of site-seeing for the travel writer to follow which focuses on monumental structures: the ruins of Sacsayhuaman in Cuzco and Sillustani near Puno; the convents and churches of Lima and Cuzco, etc. These itineraries help the writer to construe a complex map of time in which Peru is frozen in the past, whether that past involves the grandeur of the Inca civilization (exemplified by the ruins of a bygone age) disassociated from their surviving descendants or the administrative control formerly maintained by the Spanish colonial system (as evident in the architecture of the churches and administrative buildings).

This past time of an orderly yet bygone age is set apart from another past time of general "backwardness" that infects what many of the travelers considered a present time of chaos.[7] At this point, an itinerary of informal sites and sights plays an important role. Some of particular interest include the *tambos* (inns) en route to certain archeological sites; the religious festivals and street plays; the poor infrastructure of roads, etc. Here an ethnographic eye constructs a social map of Peruvian *tipos* (types of inhabitants) populating such sights/sites. An ethnographic gaze not only takes note of the *quaint* roles fulfilled or popular customs performed by these stock characters but also classifies their racial composition. The racial heterogeneity of the Peruvian society further signals a "degenerate" society as both bloodlines and social spaces blur into societal *disorder*, a disorder that sets the stage for moral mappings by the traveler regarding who should be in charge of modernizing (and ordering) Peru. This time, that signals "backwardness," intersects with the racial charting of *tipos* to justify an ethos of superiority which involves a racial and/or cultural hierarchy.

These itineraries and their subsequent mappings mark those constituted as *others*, allowing the traveler to authorize and naturalize his/her discourse. This "othering" whether by the European or United States subject in an exotic *other* land or by the Peruvian Creole (Peruvian-born descendent of Spanish parents) mapping national *others* serves each subject to construct a hierarchy in which he or she places all *others* as racially, morally, socially beneath him/her in order to laden his/her discourse with authority regarding what constitutes the Peruvian and his landscape.

Though the objects each traveler examines and constitutes in his/her travelogue are frequently similar, the motives behind the ethnographic gaze manifest themselves differently in those texts representative of imperialist empires and those texts authored by Peruvians in that, in the case of the Peruvian texts, the objects of the ethnographer's gaze often serve as riches and evidence of the nation's prosperity whereas those of the European and United States texts are used to point out the "degradation" of Peruvian society and subsequent "necessity" of European or United States intervention.

Peru, indeed, constitutes a site of dialogue in that all the travelers under study engage in certain citational practices to authorize their travelogues. They are dialogical in the sense that each one of the traveler's utterance (politically, subjectively interested) at various times reinforces the writings of previous travelers, anticipates the texts of future travelers or refutes the utterance of previous travelers to Peru. In fact, various writing subjects examined here actually refer to one another either implicitly or explicitly, sometimes agreeing with one another, sometimes correcting one another, sometimes contesting one another.

Case studies of how certain conventions are played out differently, according to each writing subject's locus of enunciation, and the resulting dialogism that takes place will be the subject of the subsequent chapters.

Chapter 3: Constructing Peru: Imperialist Representations of a "Backward" Nation

This chapter examines how travelers manipulate certain tropes in travel discourse to authorize themselves as subjects. It is divided into three areas. Each area concerns a different grouping of travel writers regarding their loci of enunciation that in turn affects their respective representations of Peruvian culture.

In the case of the European and North American travelers to Peru, their representations of Peruvian sights and sites are often alluded to in terms of "wretchedness" indicating a backwardness of infrastructure, poverty, popular customs and miscegenated inhabitants. This "wretchedness" serves as a stark contrast to the "splendor" that these travelers describe regarding monuments and vestiges of Inca rule, signs of a bygone age which indicate that the present inhabitants of Peru have been left without a civilizing and modernizing force. I will investigate how these modes of representing society naturalize the call for either capitalist investment or Western moralizing presence of Europe or North America in Peru.

The second subdivision under study in this chapter involves those intranational travel texts written by Peruvians themselves. Here I will analyze how the Creole (or even *mestizo*, of indigenous and Spanish descent in the case of Juan Bustamante) travelers also form hierarchies based on race and typological time in order to distinguish themselves as those Peruvians validated in representing, guiding and modernizing Peru. As Fabian points out this typological time has both a distancing and evaluative effect in that the object or referent is presented as living in a Time distinct and less evolved than that of the traveler's. These Peruvian writers point to the jungle areas as regions whose inhabitants are national "others" (*savages*) stuck in a backwards uncivilized time and, therefore, in need of the *limeño* or *serrano* Creole's guidance. Though the Creole writers also catalog the sites that best express the splendor of the Inca civilization, I will point out how they do so with a different purpose in mind: the Incan sites are now represented as testaments of a national culture. Whereas *tipos* described by United States or European travelers signify a "wretchedness" and a subsequent need for intervention, the *tipos* represented by the Creole travelers are, like the Incan monuments, also nationalized. They are part of a national treasury and emphasize that Peru is an autonomous nation, already well-represented by the Creole and on the path of progress by the efforts of Peruvians themselves without the need of intervention.

In the third subdivision, I analyze how both the women travelers under consideration, Tristan and Dahlgren, are also complicit in reinforcing a United States or Eurocentric discourse. In their representations of Peruvian society, they also employ a discourse laden with typological time and racialized mapping. However, I also consider how their authority involves a feminine gendered element in that upper class, white European and American women were granted moral authority and "assigned a moral mission to teach and to work for reform in the world outside of the home" (Schriber 53). The case of Flora Tristan is more problematic than that of Dahlgren since she is half-

Peruvian herself. Nevertheless, though Tristan as a writing subject does not easily fit into the imperialist's capitalist project, she does express a certain Eurocentricism and is not without race and class biases, a point which she shares with other European and United States women travelers of the period. Textual analyses and examples will concern the following texts: von Tschudi's *Travels in Peru*; Dahlgren's *South Sea Sketches*; Tristan's *Peregrinaciones*; Valdéz y Palacios' *Viaje del Cuzco*; Bustamante's *Viaje al Antiguo Mundo*; and Fuentes' *Lima*.[8]

Chapter 4: Talking Back to the Center(s)

> ¡Qué ramo de riqueza escondido en esos veinte mil quintales de lana...que anualmente nos lleva el extranjero por un precio vil, para vendérnoslos luego...! Es decir que sobre esa pérdida en nuestros propios intereses, todavía se nos sigue la ruina de nuestras fábricas...para los goces y el engrandecimiento de la industria europea.
>
> Juan Bustamante, *Viaje al Antiguo Mundo* (1849)

Talking Back to the Center(s) concentrates on the dialogical nature of travelogues through an examination of how Peruvian travel writers, finding themselves marginalized by imperialist world powers, use their travelogues to talk back to various centers. The first half of this chapter will be dedicated to a close analysis of the cross talk that takes place in travelogues produced by Peruvians in which their representations of their culture both directly and indirectly engage with those representations produced by imperialist writers. The Peruvian subjects negotiate with the Eurocentric and North American representations in the sense that they at once agree with some of those representations in an effort to authorize themselves within the travel genre but also directly contest such versions and present themselves as more authorized in presenting their own culture. This chapter points out in which situations the Peruvian contestation of imperialist representations becomes most urgent.

However, as the chapter title suggests, there is not just one center to talk back to. The second half of this chapter will involve analyzing the intranational cross talk that takes place between *limeño* and *serrano* Creoles, a tension several European travel writers during the period note in their travelogues. Those travel writers born to the Sierra region find themselves doubly marginalized both by a North American or European center as well as by that of Lima. Therefore, in this section the contestation of *limeño* misrepresentation of *serrano* culture (or the absence of the Sierra in national discourse) will also be examined. Core texts used for this section will primarily be those authored by Peruvian intellectuals: Valdéz y Palacios' *Viaje del Cuzco*; Bustamante's *Viaje al Antiguo Mundo*; and Fuentes' *Lima*.

Conclusion

Lastly, the conclusion includes a summary and synthesis of the primary points expressed in the previous chapters with the intention of reiterating how travel discourse concerning Peruvian culture is highly dialogical from a number of perspectives.

The topic of Peru hosted a bi-directional dialogue among travelers during the 1800s. The travelogues examined exhibit a double character of language in the sense that the discourse of each of the writing subjects assumes, bears in mind, or refutes the discourses of predecessor texts as well as anticipates criticism from subsequent travelogues or discussions on the topic. In examining closely how writing subjects take up and reposition themselves discursively in these travelogues I hope to pinpoint the different social accents (accents saturated with subjective and political intentions) that are exhibited in this nineteenth century dialogue and debate of what constitutes Peruvian culture, what constitutes its future, and what constitutes the writing subject's authority on the matter. Finally, I raise some questions and suggestions for further study based on my findings and analysis.

Notes

1. Besides Alison Blunt's work on this issue see also the following works: Alison Blunt and Gillian Rose's *Writing Women and Space* (1994); various essays in *Close Encounters of Empire* (1998); Sara Mill's *Discourses of Difference* (1991); Mary Louise Pratt's *Imperial Eyes* (1992); Mary Schriber's *Writing Home* (1997); David Spurr's *The Rhetoric of Empire* (1992); various articles in *Women and Imperialism* (1992); various essays in *Travellers' Tales* (1994); and Deborah Poole's *Vision, Race, and Modernity* (1997).

2. Other scholars before Pratt's work compied and anthologized travelogues written by Latin American writers as well as by European writers who traveled to Latin America. See, for example, Estuardo Núñez's exhaustive anthologizing efforts regarding travel texts about Peru. However, Núñez's anthologies do not include discursive and cultural analyses of the texts themselves.

3. Some examples of additional texts to be consulted are E. De Sartiges' *Viage a las repúblicas de América del Sur* (1851); Charles Darwin's *The Voyage of the Beagle* (1839); Clements Markham's *Cuzco and Lima* (1856); Karl Scherzer's *Visit to Peru* (1859); E.G. Squire's *Peru: Incidents of Travel and Exploration* (1877); Ida Pfeiffer's *A Lady's Second Journey around the World* (1856); and Ethel Gwendo line Vincent's *From China to Peru* (1894). As for Scherzer's text, the original version was first published in German as *Reise der Österreichischen*. E. De Sartiges' text was originally published in French: *Voyage dans les Républiques de l'Amérique du Sud*.

4. A famous arqueologist of the time from Vienna, von Tschudi's text first appeared in German under the following title: *Ueber die ureinwohner von Peru*. As for Tristan's text, it was first published in French as *Mémoires et pérégrinations d'une paria*.

5. Protectionist policies resulted from an economic philosophy less inclined toward laissez-faire trade policies.

6. Proto-feminist projects refer to those projects that "feature any ideas which would seem to be similar to the ones exhibited by...feminist texts and concerns" even though their texts preceded any real consolidated, feminist movement (Mills 29).

7. This type of split-time is known as an mode of typological time found in ethnographic discourses discussed in Johannes Fabian's, *Time and the Other: How Anthropology Makes Its Object* (1983).

8. As pertains to the Peruvian writers, Valdéz y Palacios and Bustamante represent themselves as serranos. Valdéz y Palacios is from the departamento of Cuzco, and Bustamante is from Puno; Fuentes is representative of the limeño Peruvian

• CHAPTER TWO •

Ghosts in the Machine: Citational Practices, Travel and Ideological Itineraries

> Ellos [los "Indios Guanahani"] andan todos desnudos como gente su madre los parió ...Ellos no traen armas ni las conocen, porque les mostré espadas y las tomaban por el filo, y se cortaban con ignorancia. No tienen algún hierro...
>
> Cristóbal Colón, Diario de abordo (1492)

> ...[D]e estos yungas, todo ellos tenían unos ritos y usaban unas costumbres; gastaban muchos días y noches en sus banquetes y bebidas; y cierta cosa es grande la cantidad de vino o chicha que estos indios beben, pues nunca dejan de tener el vaso en la mano.
>
> Pedro Cieza de León, La crónica del Perú (1553)

> [Lima]...is, without exception, the dirtiest [city] in South America – filth, dirt, and rubbish are to be seen in the streets all day long....The men of Lima appear to be a different race from all others I met with in South America, for they are dirty and indolent to an amazing degree...
>
> Charles Brand, Journal of a Voyage to Peru (1828)

> Era una cosa nueva para mí, hija del siglo XIX...la representación de un misterio bajo el pórtico de una iglesia, en presencia de una inmensa multitud del pueblo. Más el espectáculo más lleno de enseñanza era la brutalidad, los vestidos groseros, los harapos de ese mismo pueblo, cuya extrema y estúpida superstición retrotraían mi imaginación a la Edad Media.
>
> Flora Tristan, Peregrinaciones de una paria (1838)

Through various rhetorical modes and tropes, nineteenth-century imperialist travel writers rendered Peruvian culture *inferior* in comparison to the writers' home cultures. However, their representational language has in it a haunting rhetorical code that evokes several centuries of travel writings concerning the "New World" in general and Peru in particular.

Peering at the epigraphs presented at the onset of this chapter, one notes a code which seems to hearken to the language and rhetoric found in the chronicles and accounts about the "New World" written by Spanish explorers, conquerors, chroniclers and priests 200 and 300 years prior to the 1800s. Among the epigraphs presented, the first one, pertaining to one of Columbus' texts was not chosen solely due to when it was written, but rather because of the way it was written impacted later representations of cultures in the Americas. According to Ania Loomba, it is important to look at Christopher Columbus' arrival to the "New World," since his "arrival functions as an 'originary moment' that...is endlessly revisited by subsequent encounters" (108). Though Loomba doesn't refer specifically to Columbus' texts but rather to his arrival as an "originary moment," within the realm of trans-Atlantic travel writing, Columbus' texts act as originary *textual* moments as well with respect to representations of Americas' inhabitants as constituted through his journal and letters.

According to scholars such as Margarita Zamora and Mary Campbell, Columbus' *Diario* (as well as his letters) impacted both the genre of travel writing and influenced subsequent representations of New World cultures. For example, Campbell points out that Columbus' contribution to the genre was that of narrativity which involved adding "character and plot" to the tradition of travel writing (Campbell 186). Another crucial element that surpassed the traditionally technical and third-person mode employed in navegational logs prior to Columbus' *Diario*, was how Columbus wrote in such a way as to give "testimony of the subjective experience of the space encountered"—in other words, the traveler becomes a first-person hero-narrator of the travelogue (Zamora 124).[1] Through this hero-narrator, subjective experience comments on and represents the *other* world s/he narrates. The surveying I/Eye of witness becomes authoritative through experiential data in the sense that the traveler's gaze functions as an operation of surveillance. The writing subject gains a position of authority through all s/he sees, classifies and explains regarding an *other* culture (Pratt 74).[2]

Columbus' texts wielded a vast shelf-life of influence in the writings of subsequent travelers to Latin America, since Columbus' "interpretation of the Caribbean and the network of images on which he relied to convey it left their mark, and the old worldview refracted through his romances died hard" (204). The "mark" that he left was his representational language. Throughout his *Diario* and letters to the Crown, Columbus represented the peoples he encountered as homogenously lacking *Western* forms of vestments, institutions, architecture, religion and technology. Though he might not have imagined that such examples of *lack* were based on a Western paradigm that biased his interpretation, he, nevertheless, failed to acknowledge that he, too, brought another form of lack to the Americas: at best, his lack of awareness of (and, at worst, his lack of respect for) alternative worldviews and practices. However, considerations as to alternative worldviews and practices certainly would not have been of concern since his voyage was commissioned by the

Spanish Crown for the express purpose of royally sanctioned enterprise that was also masked discursively under the guise of a Christian Civilizing Mission.

Columbus' representations of the "Indians" he encountered, who appeared to him as "poor," "naked," and "ignorant" of working iron to fashion advanced weaponry, would become powerful descriptors in the texts of later *conquistadores*, explorers, scientists, travelers and so forth who helped to maintain notions of (or rhetorically *prove*) Western superiority over "New World" cultures.[3]

After Columbus, theories would arise (each with an underlying desire) to explain why such cultures were *un*(Westernly)*civilized*. Conjecture, then, birthed Eurocentric theories in the 1700 and 1800s—supposedly substantiated through empirical observation— that professed such peoples as uncivilized due to a (discursively constructed) *inherent inferiority*. Some such theories (as in the case of Georges Leclerc de Buffon's theories on climate) explained Latin American peoples as inferior due to the climate in which they lived; others attributed their inferiority based on the degree of miscegenation that existed among them (a theory often attributed to John Burke and Joseph-Arthur Gobineau); finally others explained such inferiority based on social evolutionary models which were birthed out of Charles Darwin's studies on evolution.

The notion of a rhetorical inheritance spans several centuries of representing the inhabitants of Latin America, from the Caribbean peoples represented by Columbus to the peoples of Peru. Whether from the sixteenth-century writings of Pedro Cieza de León or from the nineteenth-century writings of Charles Brand and Flora Tristan, among others, the inhabitants of Peru were rendered through travel writing as *superstitious, filthy, ignorant, barbaric, uncivilized* and as a people exuding a quality of *lack*. They *lacked* elements that Western cultures had to a (Westernly) *civilized* and *superior* degree. This code stems from a modern Western worldview (initiated by Western expansionist desire and invigorated by transatlantic exploration) that biased any text regarding the New World.

Travel narratives offer scholars a rich repository of textual data to consider in examining Western imperialist agendas of the nineteenth century. They also offered travel writers, themselves, a useful repository of information. Travel narratives allowed the travel-writing subject a reserve of authoritative works to consult in the construction of his/her own travel text. Travelogues, chronicles and accounts about Peru written decades, even centuries before the 1800s, offered the nineteenth-century traveler a wealth of "predecessor texts"— those texts which the traveler would consult for a variety of reasons before attempting his/her own narrative about Peru.

This is especially true when one considers the travel genre as it pertains to various nineteenth-century travel writers who traveled to Peru. For the Western traveler to nineteenth-century Peru, s/he was writing about a site that was "new" to him/her, but that site had already been written about voluminously by preceding travelers. Many travel writers cited, quoted or alluded to New World travel accounts and chronicles, which became sources for histories, philosophical and scientific texts written by English, French and U.S. intellectuals in the 1700 and 1800s.[4] Travelers who trekked to Peru during the 1800s consulted all manner of histories and travelogues about Peru prior to their own travels to the region.

For example, an important historian often cited by travelers to Peru—especially in the cases of E. George Squier and Mrs. Howard Vincent—was William H. Prescott who wrote *History of the Conquest of Peru* (1843). Prescott's work was not only consumed by readers of the U.S. and Europe, however. As Mark Thurner points out, "Prescott's two-volume work was quickly translated into Spanish and soon gained a place on the bookshelves of the Peruvian intellegentsia" (Thurner, "Peruvian Genealogies" 163). In his work, Prescott cites and quotes many Spanish chroniclers. Among others, Prescott relies especially on the chronicles and accounts written by Cieza de León, Betanzos, Acosta, and Inca Garcilaso de la Vega. Prescott also uses travelogues written by contemporaries of his time as source materials, citing, for examples, those written by Alexander von Humboldt, and W.B. Stevenson.[5] Prescott aside, several travelers to Peru such as von Humboldt, J.J. von Tschudi, and Charles Darwin also quote or cite Spanish chronicles in their travelogues. For those travelers who do not explicitly cite information from the Spanish chronicles—such as Karl Scherzer, Charles Brand and Madeleine Vinton Dahlgren they, nevertheless, quote or allude to the travelogues of their contemporaries that did cite the chronicles, which would demonstrate their familiarity with the views expressed by such chroniclers.

The above-mentioned citational practices of nineteenth-century writers demonstrates how the accounts and chronicles produced and archived from the period of "Discovery," conquest and colonization did not lose their relevance once the Crown lost its colonies to the Latin America independence movements of the early 1800s. Merely taking the nineteenth-century traveler's representation at face value as if birthed solely from a nineteenth-century Western worldview would fail to take note of the cumulative residue and authority of the tradition that nurtured it discursively over several centuries.

Building on Monique Wittig's discussion of how language as "a set of acts, repeated over time...produce reality-effects...misperceived as 'fact,'" Judith Butler points out that "evidence" through repetition accumulates to "prove natural proofs" about an *Other* (Butler 115). These citational practices shed light on how influential predecessor texts were to travelers of the 1800s. Schriber finds— in her study of nineteenth-century writings by U.S. travelers who ventured abroad—the itineraries and routes which travelers took "were not original" because they relied on predecessors who had already "clear[ed] an avenue into foreign lands" (Schriber 16; 62). The same can be said about the travelers examined in this chapter regarding imperialists who trekked to Peru. Travel writers helped build the mounting reality-effected "evidence" that Peruvians were "inherently inferior" to the imperialist travel writers themselves and the home cultures they were allegient to.

Predecessor texts also held a disciplinary influence over the travelers' writing in addition to being useful to consult for considering routes to take. Schriber writes that "[t]ravel books are compendia of obligatory talk about obligatory sites inscribed and prescribed in guidebooks and canonical literature" to such a degree that predecessor texts, such as guidebooks and other literature, contributed to "creating a textual attitude" in the writing of later travelers (Schriber 49; 65). In fact, she found that "should a traveler dare not to visit the prescribed sites or experience the prescribed sensations" a confession or explanation would ensue in the traveler's justification for not attending such sites (17).

These itineraries of sites and sights, preset by predecessor texts, bespeaks of the dialogic nature of travel writing, since the routes taken reaffirmed previous itineraries, or in Bakhtin's words, previous "verbal performances in print" (*The Dialogic* 58). Dialogism involves how an utterance (or discourse) is embodied by a socio-historical context, by previous discourse and by the anticipation of subsequent discourses. A text in print "also inevitably orients itself with respect to previous performances in the same sphere, both those by the same author and those by the other authors" because a printed verbal performance also "responds to something, objects to something, affirms something, anticipates possible responses and objections, seeks support, and so on" (58-59). For Bakhtin, utterance is dialogic in the sense that the word is not isolated from the social and ideological context in which it is uttered. Rather, it "inevitably orients itself with respect to previous performances [utterances]" in which contexts intersect one another socially and politically from different perspectives (58-59).

The dialogic nature of nineteenth-century travelogues often produces what Schriber calls "textual attitudes" that create "blind spots" in a travel-writing subject's field of vision (Schriber 65). Therefore, travelers often "do *not* set out to see a sight empirically; rather, they undertake to find the congruence of a sight with the idea of it, with a type that derives from earlier travelers" (65).

However, *blind spot* is a term that divorces the travel writer from any complicity on his/her part and ignores that travel writers were often willing purveyors of imperialist ideology and supporters of imperialist agendas. *Blind spot* bypasses the power dynamics involved in the writing subject's desire to write from a position of *superiority* over the *others* s/he represents in his/her text.

To underscore the dynamics of power, I will borrow from Schriber's use of prescribed itineraries, but I will supplement the term with the word, "travel," and opt for the term *prescribed travel itineraries*. I supplement it in this way to offset it from an additional term I've coined, *prescribed ideological itineraries*. *Prescribed travel itineraries* denotes the physical routes and stops at particular sites and sights, the *what* the traveler sets out to see. These routes and stops allow for places to collect the supposed "raw data" or empirical data from which emantes and ideologically-charged narration of such data. As for the term, *prescribed ideological itineraries*, I will refer to them to examine the point at which travelers "undertake to find the congruence of a sight with the idea of it, with a type that derives from earlier travelers" (65). In other words, *prescribed ideological itineraries* conform to the ideological narration of what is seen, in which what is viewed is processed through the use of tropes, primarily through the tropes of metaphor and metonymy. The "prescribed" nature of these itineraries does not abolish a travel-writer's agency in adjusting itineraries to fit their own personal, narrative and political agendas to some degree, however.

Though Scriber finds that conventional constraints regarding appropriate itineraries produce moments of authorial anxiety in the writing-subject who failed to stop at a particular desitination, I suggest that the discursive strategies used by travel writers to justify the bypassing of a particular site demonstrate both moments of anxiety and agency to overcome them. A few examples might suffice to demonstrate how the travel-writing subject is not overdetermined by conventional constraints. For example, many travelers to Peru narrate their reservations about viewing bullfights and trying to refuse invitations without seeming discourteous as guests or neglecting their duty as travel-writers. Tristan maintains that she managed to resist many times but finally acquiesces due to her interest in studying the country's customs (Tristan 266). In the cases of Scherzer and Dahlgren, they avoid the spectacle all together—each with their own strategies to excuse their need to do so. Scherzer refers the reader to von Tschudi's travelogue, explaining to the reader that von Tschudi's description should suffice, and, therefore, there is no need for Scherzer to assume the task himself (Scherzer 100). Dahlgren's convenient mode of justifying her decision not to attend the bullfights is to point out that they have lost their popularity with the "best society" who "no longer give it prestige by their presence to any great extent" (Dahlgren 44).

In the cases of Peruvian regional travelers such as Juan Bustamante and José Manuel Valdéz y Palacios, they forge new itineraries altogether as a form of protest. Frustrated by the prescribed travel itineraries many imperialist travel writers followed, generally leaving out discussions about the Peruvian *departamentos* of Puno and Cuzco, they argue that leaving out such stops limits any adequate discussion or representation of Peruvian culture. Their manipulation of the conventional prescribed travel itinerary through Peru exemplifies a discernable and subversive moment of agency that Judith Butler terms an *iterative shift* (Butler, *Gender* 145). *Iterative shifts* or "strategies of subversive repetition" occur when the writing subject is able to achieve "a repetition of [a] discursive law" that in some way does not serve to consolidate it, but rather displace it (30).

The prescriptive nature of itineraries that Shriber rightly points out certainly encouraged the possibility of blind spots clouding a traveler's vision. However, it would be remiss to think such blind spots in travel writing occur through mere happenstance of genre constraints themselves. More than genre constraints are at issue here when considering imperialist agendas and travel writers' complicity in supporting them. The ideological underpinnings in the imperialist travel-writing subject's configuration of a sight in such a way that would match the *sightings* of travelers before him/her have real consequences. They reinforced a discourse that served to posit imperialist superiority over those found in *other* lands.

Considering the dialogic nature of travel writing as a "printed verbal performance" helps one to better discern the haunting quality behind negative representations of Peru and its people, which reoccur over centuries. The accumulated "truth" of representations and theories proffered by one generation of thought bequeathed a machinery of representation to new generations, fortified by new expansionist desires hence, the title of this chapter, Ghosts in the Machine. Having found a *haunting* quality in travel writing myself while studying travelogues about nineteenth-century Peru, the title of Dennis Porter's *Haunted Journeys* drew my attention. His book analyzes European travelogues from a psychoanalytical framework. It underscores a Freudian sense of the Uncanny in the travel-writing subject's encounter with an *Other* world. That is to say that Porter finds in the traveling subject's discourse a connection between "the search for origins" and its implication "that love of 'place' is prior to love for a human object, that it is, in fact, homesickness for the lost world of prenatality" (Porter 12). Therefore, the "desire to leave a given home is at the same time the desire to recover an original lost home" which, according to Porter, produces an haunting effect of dèjá vu. This quality of dèjá vu appears most prominently when "in extra-European travel writing...the traveler reports on the sensation of coming face to face in a remote place with the apparent past of the human race in its pristineness or menace" (12). While Porter's work is useful, there is also another form of rattling the chains (so-to-speak) in the travel-writer's construction of his/her narrative from a cultural and discursive analysis which is important to consider.

To examine the rhetorical ghosts that haunt the representations of nineteenth-century Peru and Peruvians in the travel texts written by imperialist writers, the first part of this chapter entails a genealogical exploration of Western discourses that converged to constitute the Other. Doing so allows one to discern the layers of discourse that imbue codified terms such as *superstitious, indolent, savage*, etc. (as exhibited in the epigraphs at the onset of the chapter) found in nineteenth-century representations of post-independent Peru. Taking into account the Eurocentric discourses discussed in the first section of the chapter and their reproductive value, the second portion of the chapter involves cultural and discursive analyses of the representations of nineteenth-century Peruvian culture that were written by travelers from the U.S. and Western Europe. These analyses include an examination of the prescribed travel itineraries that those travelers followed and the ideological itineraries that saturate their narratives.

Western Desires and Burdens of Authority: Colonial and Imperialist Expansionism and the Discursive Need for the New World and Peruvian Other

Throughout history from the period of conquest to that of post-independence Latin America, travelogues offered Western travelers a compelling textual space through which to revise and perform a Western script. Though the actors, the discursive props, delivery and desires changed throughout the years, each revised script regenerated a continuous finale of Western superiority. The Western subject constituted him/herself as superior world adventurer through discourse, while s/he discursively fashioned the New World inhabitant as inferior. Yet, as writing-subject, s/he could not control the rules of discursive engagement, so that the subject (only appearing *masterful*) would have to discursively reconfigure his/her position to maintain a guise of superiority. This need for discursive reconfiguration helps explain why negatively charged terms such as *indolent* and *superstitious* take on different discursive layers from period to period, though simultaneously borrowing from previous representations.

For example, in the Spanish texts of New World encounters and early colonization the term *superstitious* represented the indigenous Peruvians who practiced their own native religions. They were *superstitious* due to their being either incognizant of Christianity or unwilling to follow it once made aware of its teachings. Yet, that same descriptor expands in representational possibility for the imperialist travel writers of the 1800s. Looking at the epigraph taken from Flora Tristan's travelogue, one finds that the term *superstitious* (and all its variant uses) becomes a term capable of subsuming all manner of believers. The term can include those who practice native religions or those who practice a popular form of Catholicism in churches, which the travelers found were managed and decorated contrary to a Western European/Protestant code of religious aesthetics that gravitated toward more of a sense of austerity in terms of how to celebrate and in terms of how to ornament the churches' interiors. This is largely due to the fact that many of the imperialist writers were protestant and/or adherents of liberalism's insistence on the separation of Church and State.

The appropriation of such descriptors and the extension of their applicability to largely all inhabitants of post-independent Peru, nevertheless, hearken to older voices. For this reason, the first part of this chapter entails a genealogical exploration of Western discourses that converged to constitute the Peruvian as Other (Foucault, *Archaeology* 78). Doing so allows one to discern the layers of discourse that imbue codified terms such as *superstitious*, *indolent*, *savage*, etc., found in nineteenth-century representations of post-independent Peru. Such an exploration fosters a better insight into how the observational "facts" in a non-fictional (and, therefore, supposedly *transparent*) genre about Peruvian culture proffered by nineteenth-century imperialist traveler-writers carried with them the voices and beliefs of those before them while simultaneously appropriating those voices to fit new agendas.

Spanish Desire in the "New World" From Columbus to Colonial Peru
A travel through representations of "New World" *Others* and the capitalist desires that provided the undercurrent for those representations begins with Columbus and his texts as originary textual moments and how they impacted trans-Atlantic travel narratives. Columbus' texts are important in terms of how they influenced the genre of travel writing as it related specifically to the "New World." They are also important due to the socio-political context, the Western Renaissance, during which they were produced. During the Western Renaissance two important Western discourses converged: the religious discourse of Christianity played counterpoint to the political and economic discourse of capitalism.

In terms of travel narratives regarding the "New World," Columbus' texts continued several Western literary and/or oral traditions which involve a heroic adventurer-protagonist embattling or encountering a notorious *Other*. For example, Mary Campbell notes that Greco-Roman writers passed on the notion of all things *monstrous* found in a world *Other* than their own—in the case of the Ancients, the *monstrous* East. They and their "medieval inheritors...continued what had become a traditional identification of monsters with the East..." (Campbell 48). From writers such as Ctesias and Herodotus, the medieval travel books that followed had in them the lore of the *monstrous* East which carried on into the Western imaginary of subsequent generations of explorers. Another tradition, the *romance*, also involves an heroic protagonist encountering an *Other*. The tradition of the *romance* was born out of the centuries-long Spanish Reconquest and subsequent defeat of the Moors. The *romance*'s plot follows the trials of a heroic Christian adventurous hero bound to "defeat any manner of monstrous events or altercations with an exoticized, non-Christian other, more-specifically the Moorish infidel" (Jara and Spadaccini 7). Encountering idolaters in the *New* World would plug into *Old* World notions of the monstrously Moorish infidel.

Beyond supplanting himself in his travelogue as protagonist, the new Christian adventurer, Columbus' attention to describing the natural landscape and inhabitants helped revitalize an intellectual discussion that was popular among Greco-Roman writers: how a human's natural surroundings affected his/her human condition and stature. Gerbi, in his *The Dispute of the New World*, examines how theories about the influence of nature and climate on a people have had a continual history traced back to the Ancients of the Classical period. For instance, he finds that Greek and Roman writers Aristotle, Herodotus, Cicero and Plato among them all related climate to a people's "spirit" (36).

Columbus' texts are also important in that they add to the new Christian-adventure a hero who is commissioned officially by the Spanish Crown to scour the landscape for potential profit to the empire he was representing. It is important to remember that during Columbus' time, "Europe was suffering a severe shortage of monetary metals...and most European nations were possessed of gold coinages by the middle of the fourteenth century" (Campbell 183). Searching for gold drove both Columbus' narratives as well as his itinerary.

Campbell writes that travel is born of a "*collision* between inherited and experienced knowledge" (Campbell 165; emphasis mine). With an analysis of Columbian texts, however, one might be inclined to add also that it becomes more obvious during the Western Age of Discovery that travel can be viewed as a *collusion of inherited and experienced knowledge*. It was a collusion nourished by desire on the part of the individual and the nation-state.

The Spanish trans-Atlantic "exploration," conquest and colonization of the Americas involved a symbiotic relationship between the commissioned explorer/conquistador and the Spanish Crown. It was a relationship that benefited both. On the part of the traveling individual, the Americas served as an opening to improve one's lot more easily than he/she could in Spain. The increased possibility to improve one's status and wealth provided a desire on an individual level that, likewise, supported the Crown's agenda. This symbiosis encouraged a "nobility and would-be nobility anxious for more conquests, and a crown ready to direct these subjects overseas...[T]here is considerable evidence to suggest that the New World conquerors...came to America in order to win social status as well as wealth" (Skidmore and Smith 15-16).

Columbus was no exception. Since he was appointed as Admiral, Viceroy, and Governor-General, the Crown assured him the opportunity to enjoy "one-tenth of all the treasure and merchandise produced or obtained" in the territories he "discovered" on behalf of the Crown (Greenblatt 57). Columbus' letters to the Crown and the *Diario* (his log which detailed his first voyage to the Indies) serve as texts that attest to the desire underlying the representation of the *Other* and his writings were accounts written to and required by the Spanish Crown—"upon whose whim...exploration wholly depended" (Campbell 175).

As accounts they have in them what Campbell finds to be "a mixture of official report and propaganda" (165). Therefore, they act as "guilty texts" because they "played a large part in the developments of...European colonialism, and they helped to establish the basis for a 'justified' Christian imperialism" (166). Campbell underscores that the "Discovery of the New World" was not an innocent adventure for the travel-curious but rather a traveling venture for the profit-minded:

> Columbus knew from the start that he went in search of the Indies, of gold, and of Christian converts, all at once...And the order in which they succeed each other as focuses of attention is natural: the first step is physically to find the Indies, the next to find gold, and when that material object begins to appear elusive, it is politic of him to concentrate on the spiritual profit Ferdinand and Isabella may reap from his expeditions. (198)

One document that illustrates these interconnected desires is a letter Columbus wrote to Luis de Santángel, dated February 15, 1493. Luis de Santángel was an official of the Crown of Aragon "who had been instrumental in facilitating the Columbian enterprise" (Zamora 10). Margarita Zamora in her book *Reading Columbus*, points out that this letter (along with another sent out on the same date almost entirely in duplicate form to another Crown official) is of paramount importance because it was "so vigorously and widely circulated" as if "part of a concerted propaganda campaign" (11). Both letters were used to announce the "Discovery."

In his letter to Luis de Santángel, Columbus assures the official that he has taken possession in the name of their Highnesses of the areas of the Indies that he's discovered: "..[v]os escribo esta, por la cual sabréis cómo en 33 días pasé a las Indias con la armada que los ilustrísimos Rey y Reina, nuestros señores, me dieron, donde yo hallé muchas islas pobladas..., y dellas todas he tomado posesión por sus Altezas..." (Colón 222). After Columbus reports that the first goal of finding the Indies and taking possession of them for the Crown has been achieved, he then provides an inventory of all things and persons found: abundant resources to exploit and market, now under Spain's rule. Touring through *La Española* (what is today the island of two nations, Haiti and the Dominican Republic), Columbus describes the lands there with an eye turned toward future economic potential for Spain: "...[S]on fertilísimas en demasiado grado...; en ella hay muchos puertos en la costa de la mar sin comparación de otros que yo sepa en cristianos, y hartos ríos...y llenas de árboles..." (223).

After describing the lay of the land, his next sentence, and the paragraph that proceeds it, involves a more mercantilistic gaze. For example, he writes of the resources that are of *inestimable* value (which he took possession of, lest we forget) the metal mines and a rich labor force: "En las tierras hay muchas minas de metales y hay gente de inestimable número..." (223). The paragraph that then ensues highlights other resources which present more possibilities for reaping benefit from such lands: "La Española es maravilla:...las tierras tan hermosas y gruesas para plantar..., para criar ganados de todas suertes, para edificios de villas..." (223).

With the obvious allure of fertile lands to sow and harvest and metals to mine, Columbus turns to yet another resource. Columbus begins to introduce to his majesties, in a more detailed fashion, their new labor force of soon-to-be Christianized subjects:

> La gente desta isla y de todas las otras que he hallado y habido he noticia, *andan todos desnudos*, hombres y mugeres, así como sus madres los paren...*Ellos no tienen hierro ni acero ni armas* ni son para ello...No tienen otras armas salvo las armas de las cañas...Y...se harán cristianos, que se inclinan al amor y servicio de Sus Altezas y de toda la nación castellana...,*y nos dar de las cosas que tienen en abundancia que nos son necesarias.* (224; emphasis mine)

Columbus' representation of the *Other* peoples that he found became influential to subsequent travelers, historians and philosophers, especially his descriptions of them as a *naked* people, some obviously as an *idolatrous* people because those were the ones tagged for future slaves, and as a *poor* people who had very little in riches though they lived in fertile lands replete with metals to mine. He describes them as a people *ignorant* of iron, and steel and, therefore, *ignorant* of protecting themselves with anything more precise and mighty than reed weaponry. Importantly, they were also a people who were not yet *saved* by Christ. The signifiers of *ignorance, idolatry, poverty*, and a lack of proper *attire* were signifiers easily manipulated to *mark* such a people as *inferior*.

Yet, Columbus, did not just describe the wondrous land and *Other* peoples he found, he also provided a curious note about the indescribable, the *inestimable*, the flora and fauna that remained unidentifiable because he had little to compare it to. For instance, the coastal seaports are *sin comparación* (without comparison) and he's heard it said that the trees *jamás pierdan la hoja*, never loose their foliage which can only be compared to trees in Spain during a perpetual month of May (223-224). The lore and allure of the *monstrous* in the East converts into a lore and allure of the *marvilloso* (the marvelous) in the Indies. The Indies involves a land of miraculous abundance that remains difficult to classify but abounds unattended to.

In the postscript to his letter Columbus leaves a tantalizing morsel for the ambitious naturalists of the Enlightenment to consider in their future endeavors to identify, quantify and qualify whatever might await their scrutiny in the Americas. In this postscript, Columbus comments on the climate that seemed constantly temperate except for a rare occasion during which a storm detained his voyage for approximately two weeks: "En todas las Indias he siempre hallado los temporales como en mayo...salvo que estas tormentas me han detenido XIII días" (229). Curious about this tempestuous stint, Columbus obtains from the inhabitants that even such weather was an aberration of what they were generally accustomed to for their winter (229).

Having "discovered" a *New World*, efforts to colonize the land corresponded required further discursive ploys to reproduce the *Other* and, likewise, reproduce Spain's justification for control over the area. Though Columbus' log concerning his first voyage to this New World, represented the indigenous peoples—though with some exceptions as Edenic natives; Spanish chronicles of the sixteenth and seventeenth centuries helped reproduce the *Other*. Columbus' mercantilist gaze concentrated itself primarily on the natural landscape and the resources with a keen eye to future profit. Chroniclers still detailed the landscape but also supplemented their texts with detailing and commenting on the native peoples' behaviors, especially those behaviors that would rhetorically mark their *sinfulness* and *need* for conversion.

Among those writers who chronicled the conquest as it pertained to Peru, two of the repeatedly quoted, cited or alluded to by nineteenth-century imperialist travel writers were Pedro Cieza de León's *La crónica del Perú* (1553) and Inca Garcilaso de la Vega's *Comentarios reales* (1608). As predecessor texts these chronicles yielded a wealth of descriptors and tropes of othering that were borrowed and adjusted (appropriated) by imperialist travel-writers who ventured to Peru during the 1800s.

A brief look into how those predecessor texts were useful to nineteenth-century travel writers seems appropriate at this point, beginning with Cieza de León's text.

For Cieza de León many of the natives' idolatrous acts and sinful behaviors alike center around how the natives (those he considers the "yungas") believed their dead remained as living spirits in an *other* world (other than the Christian kingdom of heaven) where they could continue behaviors, sinful in the eyes of the Spanish Christians.[6] He writes: "Y así...era dicho opinión general en todos estos indios yungas, y aún en los serranos...que las ánimas de los difuntos no morían, sino que para siempre vivían, y se juntaban allá en el otro mundo...adonde...creían que se holgaban y comían y bebían, que es su prinicipal gloria" (162). This belief in the deceased who do not die, along with the burial practice of entumbing women alive along with the deceased, were evidence to Cieza de León that these people had been "engañados por el demonio" (162). One of those practices most inflammatory was sacrificing the loved ones of the deceased by entombing them alive with the deceased:

> Por las cuales dichos y ilusiones del demonio, ciegos estos indios, teniendo por ciertas aquellas falsas apariencias, tienen más cuidado en aderezar sus sepulcros o sepulturas que ninguna otra cosa. Y muerto el señor, le echan su tesoro, y mujeres vivas...y otras personas con quien él tuvo, siendo vivo, mucha amistad. (162)

The "principal glory" of idleness and the imbibing of the living spirits corresponded to what Cieza de León deemed typical of those *indios ciegos* still living in the flesh, for at their banquets and celebrations, Cieza de León underscores the consumption of alcohol ("vino o chicha"), since they "gastaban muchos días y noches en sus banquetes y bebidas; y cierto cosa es grande la cantidad de vino o chicha que estos indios beben, pues nunca dejan de tener el vaso en la mano" (161).[7]

Nevertheless, Cieza de León considers these people to be reformable through the Christianizing Mission: "Y ahora en nuestro tiempo, como ya vayan dejando los más de sus ritos, y el demonio no tenga fuerza ni poder...van entendiendo sus engaños y procuran de no ser tan malos como lo fueron antes que oyesen la palabra del sacro Evangelio" (162). Though Cieza de León expresses respect for the Inca system of government; believes in the worthiness of the natives once they accept conversion to Christianity; and even condemns the Spanish mistreatment of the natives; he, nevertheless, continues the mercantilist gaze of wealth the Peru offers to the Crown. As regards the region of the Andean sierras, he inventories the great deposits of silver, gold, copper, iron, and writes that "todos los metales que Dios crió es bien proveído este reino" (245).

Inca Garcilaso, a first-generation *mestizo* who lived most of his life in Spain, also describes and comments on the idolatrous *indios* within the Peruvian reign, but he also qualifies that theses practices were attributed to those *indios* not yet enlightened by the Inca conquest of the region.[7] In fact, according to Garcilaso, the Incas paved the way for Christian evangelization. He argues this by making a distinction between pre-Inca peoples and Inca peoples in terms of two historical periods previous to the Spanish Conquest so that the reader will not confuse the practices of one period with those of the more developed Inca period "para que no se confunda lo uno con lo otro ni se atribuyan las costumbres ni los dioses de los unos a los otros" (Garcilaso 26). In making this distinction Garcilaso refers to the pre-Inca peoples as little more than "bestias mansas" or, worse, who acted as "fieras bravas" (26-27): the *indios* of the first period dressed like *animales* and lived in a disorderly fashion like "bestias irracionales" before the "Imperio de los Incas" (33). Most importantly, however, is that Manco Cápac installed, according to Garcilaso, the Sun as the only god to receive idolatrous worship and designated the god, Pachacámac as the true god to celebrate "internally" (67).

For Garcilaso, the Inca rule enlightened the pre-Inca's religious ways to such degree that the number of idols worshipped were reduced to one, el Sol. And to see one god as supreme, Pachacámac. This was thanks to the first Inca, Manco Cápac who put the Inca monarchy of the Inca Kings in place. Order was established with this monarchy turning *aquellos indios* [preincaicos] into subjects. Garcilaso contends that Manco Cápac taught his vassals how to construct houses and cultivate the land and gave them laws by which to live.

This highlighting of two periods of indigenous ways in what would become the viceroyalty of Peru under the Spanish, allows Garcilaso to make an important corrective to previous Spanish chroniclers: "Los españoles aplican otros muchos dioses a los Incas por no saber dividir los tiempos y las idolatrías de aquella primera edad y las de la segunda" (67). Yet, his corrective does not preclude him from *othering* non-Inca peoples.

Both of these chronicles would become enormously important predecessor texts to consult for many nineteenth-century travelers and historians who wrote about Peru. They, like other predecessor texts, provided a repository of rhetorical strategies and representational signs of the *Other*. However, they would have to be appropriated in such a way as to fit new agendas once Spain's control of its colonies had fallen due to the independence movements in the early 1800s. Just as the project of Spanish conquest and colonization needed an *Other* to justify itself, so, too, did imperialist agendas. The rhetorical ploys which served Spanish representations of constituting the indigenous peoples as idle, superstitious, ignorant *Other* were used for a new all-inclusive *Other*—all manner of Peruvians: indigenous, *mestizo*, and Creole alike. Even the inclusion on the part of the Spanish chroniclers of the Spanish abuses would be manipulated—perpetuating the Black Legend in order to condemn Peruvians born of Spanish parents.[8] Inca Garcilaso's laudatory praise of the Inca rule and detail of various Inca religious and administrative structures and policies; the inventories of natural resources for potential wealth by other chroniclers like Cieza de León; as well as the mention of species of natural life still unclassified would encourage the traveler of the 1800s to examine Peru for him/herself. Chronicles such as those by Inca Garcilaso and Cieza de León formed a useful repository of representations to pick and choose from and transform into new ways to rhetorically mask new desires into a new civilizing mission.

Imperialist Desire in Spanish America and the Newly Independent Nations

During the 1500s, Spain, for the most part, had managed to guard and monopolize the riches it reaped from its colonies through strict protectionist trade policies. However, by the 1600 and 1700s, Spain was plagued with frequent economic instability due to several key events that lessened its revenue and stature as a dominating European power. These events included the English's victory of the Armada in 1588; Portugal's "reasserted independence" from Spanish control, which had lasted from 1588-1640; and the War of Spanish Succession during the 1700s. All of these events affected the Spanish royal treasury to the degree that it "repeatedly went bankrupt" (Skidmore 21). Particularly damaging was the result of the War of Spanish Succession. With the Bourbons assuming the Spanish throne, the British gained "the contract (asiento) for the slave trade to the Spanish colonies" (21). While Spain saw its power disintegrating, other European powers such as England and France viewed Spanish America as a site to covet for their own potential power.

Once Spain lost its control over the colonies, the newly independent nations would find themselves economically and politically vulnerable. This was partly due to the way Spain administered its colonies and what purpose they were to serve. Spain's primary interest in its colonies pertained to exploiting the resources of the colonies to enrich the royal treasury rather than to develop the colonies. Generally the infrastructure in the colonies was minimal and not well-maintained and the administrative institutions were installed in the center of its viceroyalties—the first two established pertaining to present-day Mexico City and Lima, Peru. Another problem for the precarious independent nations was how to recover from the recent diminishment of revenue through commerce and trade. Prior to the independence movements "[c]ommerce with Spain had stopped, and trade among the former colonies was also greatly reduced" (37). Therefore, the newly independent nations found they had "to deal with public debts, even before they could attempt to rebuild their economies"—which forced these new nations to look to foreign lenders (37).

Imperialist nations were eager to take advantage of these newly-independent colonies' precarious economic and political state. Peru, known for its rich deposits of metals, generated a great deal of interest for what its "potencialidad económica" (Nuñez, *Los viajeros* 7). During the 1820s and 1830s, travelers representing the U.S., England and France were often commissioned to report on Peru's economic potential. These reports were to provide "informaciones precisas sobre la suerte presente y futura del país, su situación social y su *potencialidad económica* y los viajeros las proporcionan desde diversos ángulos de apreciación" (7).

Those travelers who were not commissioned also produced (though in less detailed and formal fashion) inventories regarding Peru's natural resources. Popular travelers, such as Charles Brand, functioned as informal surveyors. They often explicitly offered up their texts as a form of national donations. In the case of Brand, he writes in his introduction that he originally offered up his travelogue "solely for the information and amusement of my friends, without any view to publication"; however, he was convinced by others to publish it because it could be useful to others (Brand v-vi). How exactly could his narrative serve others? Brand answers that in it some might find "some information useful to those, whose *business* or pleasure may lead them to pursue the paths which I have so recently trodden" (vi; emphasis mine).

Others, women and men alike, offer commentary underscoring how their nations are not taking advantage of new markets to exploit. Flora Tristan suggests that France seriously consider French wine as a lucrative product to export to Peru (195-196); Pfeiffer turns an American lack of competition into a possible future American business endeavor: "An English company has hitherto enjoyed the monopoly of the [steamer] line from Panama to Valparaiso, undisturbed by any competition from the Americans...I can not deny that I should be very glad to see some rival American steamer started" (335). De Sartiges, like other travelers, offers information regarding how France should best approach trade with Peru. For example, he suggests France consider more attentively the wool industry: "Sería un gran regalo para nuestras manufacturas de paños importar vicuñas a Francia y nada sería más fácil..." (9). Squier, formerly commissioned purchasing agent in Peru for the U.S. government during the 1860s, concentrates on one resource in particular. After listing other lucrative resources—tin, copper, wool, sugar and cotton —he particularly points out the usefulness of Peruvian cinchona bark. Squire writes that the cinchona bark could become especially lucrative and "useful to mankind" because it is a source from which to manufacture the drug, quinine (587). In its usefulness to "mankind," it is useful to U.S. commercial interests as well. In von Tschudi's examination of Peru's topography and farming, von Tschudi underscores what kinds of European crops would thrive in Peruvian soil (127-130).

Textual examples such as these demonstrate that nineteenth-century travel writers were indeed purveyors of the capitalist interest of imperialism. Yet, regardless of whether or not authors such as these explicitly offer obvious textual examples of enterprising interests and suggestions for national commerce which correspond to those of their nation's desires, they are implicitly complicit with imperialist agendas. The privilege of their authoritative gaze and the subsequent narrative they produced helped to "preserv[e], on a material and human level, the relations of power inherent in the larger system of order" (Spurr 17). In their need to establish the cultural/moral superiority of the nations the traveler-writers, themselves, represent a rhetorical need to produce the Peruvian other(s) as too *indolent, ignorant, chaotic* or *inept* to function autonomously as a progressive, orderly nation. They would borrow key descriptors of the periods of the Spanish conquest and colonialism, such as *indolent, superstitious, ignorant* but they would also become charged with the surge of new Western discourses of cultural superiority. Though foregoing somewhat the descriptor *savage*, others were quick to fill in the void with those of *semi-civilized* or *backward*.

Before presenting "new evidence" of old notions about the *Other*, the writing subject also needed to authorize him/herself as worthy and authoritative as a reliable source. This meant, to a great degree, constructing this authority through citational practices that underscored how well-read s/he was on the subject/object of Peru.

The Burden of Authorial Authority (Citational Chains and Practices and Production Constraints)

Bearing in mind the influence and authority predecessor texts provided to the traveler, one senses the accumulated residue of Eurocentric discourses that helped produce certain formulae of travel narrative conventions and itineraries regarding Peru during the 1800s. The accumulating residue of Western travel writers' perceptions of non-European cultures gained increasing validity through the frequent reiteration of previous perceptions by other Eurocentric writers (whether scholarly or popular), thus adding to a weighty sense of truth value. What I consider to be the accumulative residue of Western traveler's rhetoric and itineraries involves both an implicit and explicit regeneration of "citation chains" as part of the travel writer's effort to prove his/her authority on the subject matter, whether through reaffirming the assertions given by their contemporaries or through the published works of noted travelers a generation before them. This discursive urge to appear authoritative through the works of those writing subjects before them, who already achieved such authority, sheds light on production constraints.

As Porter points out, dialogic "hauntings" are often overt in travel writings. The overtness (through frequent citations or allusions to predecessor texts) is due in part to the "boom" of travel writing that occurred in the nineteenth century to such an extent that "the anxiety of travel writing" functions as an additional anxiety to contend with beyond the customary anxiety one has upon traveling abroad (Porter 12). Schriber notes several transformations in the early 1800s that converged in producing the boom of the genre as it pertained to U.S. travel-writers: economic prosperity, steam-powered liners and railroads as well as advancements in print technology, and, importantly, "public interest in foreign lands" (Schriber 4-5). So great was the genre's boom that women travelers were successful as well, since women's travelogues were being published serially with some degree of regularity along side those travel texts written by their male contemporaries by 1830 (2). Though Schriber focuses on travel writing and print culture as they pertained to the U.S., the same factors applied in other imperialist nations.

The power of production constraints and informational heritage becomes clearer if one examines "citation chains" used by a writing subject in an effort to build his/her authority (Hamilton 16). Richard Hamilton has explored social psychological studies which "indicate that...[a] range of extraintellectual factors is operating: tendencies toward conformity and deference to 'authority,' or to persons or texts having the appearance of authority. Nowhere is this more evident than in the scholarly habit of citing previous work to establish intellectual credibility" (16). Because the Western travel writer was writing in a genre growing ever more popular by the mid 1800s, the travelogues I've gathered demonstrate an anxiety to "conform" and "defer" at times, while adding correctives at other times. Travel and academic writers acted as an intellectual community dialoguing with one another's texts or studies, often to establish their own authority as well-versed on the subject. Albeit briefly at times, travelers frequently cited the studies of one another because writing an *authoritative* travelogue required a knowledgeable voice. They also repeated the itineraries of previous travelers.

Prescribed Travel Itineraries and Ideological Itineraries

One practical reason for consulting predecessor texts was that they helped the travel writing subject build his/her knowledgeable voice for the narration of his/her travelogue. Predecessor texts were also useful in that they helped the traveler plot an itinerary based on the writings of previous travels. According to the *Chambers Dictionary of Etymology*, *itinerary* has a direct connection to a reliance on predecessor texts, since the term comes "from the idea of using someone else's previous account as a guide for one's own travels" (Barnhart 547-548). Interestingly, this notion of itineraries drawn from previous accounts, in fact, solidified in usage during the 1800s (548).

Mary Schriber uses the term "prescribed itineraries" to refer to the nineteenth-century traveler's tendency to follow the same itineraries previous travelers took to the same locale (16-17). Though Schriber was not studying imperialist travel writing that concerned Peru, the same tendency holds true for those travelers who wrote about post-independent Peru, especially if one examines the sameness of the sites and sights that they incorporated in their texts.

According to Schriber, this sameness of itineraries created a repeated field of vision, which resulted in a narrowness of sites and sights incorporated in the traveler's experience and travelogue. As a result of this narrowed field of vision, Schriber notes that "blind spots" occur due to the traveler's effort "to find the congruence of a sight with the idea of it, with a type that derives from earlier travelers" (65). However, in an attempt to highlight the power dynamic involved in representing Peru and how the imperialist travel imbued those sites and sights in such a way as to convey the "backwardness" of Peru as a nation, I offer the term, ideological intineraries. Prescribed itineraries provided the opportunity to gather what would look to be (through the supposed transparency of an objective and non-fictional account) the raw data (the arquitecture, the manners and customs of the people, the administrative policies of the government, etc.) for describing Peru. But, at the point in which the traveler transforms the "raw data" into (constructed) "proofs" of an inferior nation, ideological itineraries come into discursive play.

Ideological itineraries involve using tropes, or figurative devices to convey meaning in such a way as to fortify imperialist discourse. Hayden White reminds us that tropes involve figurative language employed in such a way as to invoke connections among things that are not "normally" expected (White, *Tropics* 2). This comes from the idea of a "turn" in meaning which approximates "not only a deviation *from* one possible, proper meaning, but also a deviation *toward* another meaning, conception, or ideal of what is right and proper *and true* 'in reality'" (2). Two tropes that are found most commonly applied in the imperialist travel texts are those of metaphor and metonymy.

Metaphor works in such a manner as to shift a word or phrase "from its normal uses to a context where it evokes new meaning" (Preminger and Brogan 760). Though generally a metaphor is viewed poetically as a substitution of a noun for another noun, other parts of speech (such as verbs, adverbs and adjectives) are not excluded from metaphorical turns (762). A fitting example of this is von Humboldt's description of the streets in Lima as streets that are "adornadas de perros y burros muertos" (von Humboldt 86). His use of the adjectival descriptor of "adornadas" allows the phrase to convey two things; one, that Lima is a filthy and unsanitary city; and, secondly, that Lima is surrounded by a farsical sense of aesthetics.

Metonymy occurs when one word is substituted for another on the basis of some material, causal or *conceptual relation* (783; emphasis mine). I underscore the importance of *conceptual relation* because it is that mode of metonymic substitution that occurs most frequently in the travelogues under study for our purposes. In this type of metonymic turn, concrete entities (the "raw data" gathered up and facilitated by prescribed travel itineraries) are then turned to convey the abstract "essence" of Peruvian character and culture. For example, the bullfight, as viewed by von Tschudi, is not merely a diversion but becomes a sign of a "national disgrace": "Though [bullfights] form a part of Peru's national customs, they are nevertheless a national disgrace" (109). That "essence" relates primarily to summations of Peru's "inferiority" *in essence* as a modern nation.

In the language of poetics, the trope becomes the "vehicle" that suggests the "tenor" or underlying idea conveyed (760). However, in imperialist travel narrative (which is masked by a genre that presents itself as non-fictional) more is at stake than the mere play with literary devices, which White points out:

> Every mimetic text can be shown to have left something out of the description of its object or to have put something into it that is inessential to what *some* reader, with more or less authority, will regard as an adequate description….Every mimesis can be

shown to be distorted and can serve, as an occasion for yet another description of the same phenomenon, one claiming to be more realistic, more 'faithful to the facts.' (*Tropics* 3)

In terms of imperialist representations of nineteenth-century Peru, travel narratives served to construct the *reality effect* of an "inferior" Peru, which was then consumed by Eurocentric readerships as the "reality" of Peru's being an "inferior" state in the world theater.

To limit the scope of this examination of sites and sights, we will concentrate on the cities most often incorporated and which offered the travelers a view into the diverse ethnic and racial composition of the inhabitants and the customs they practiced. These cities include primarily Callao, Lima and Arequipa. More so than other cities, these three were given the most textual space and duration. They provided a wealth of "data" through which the travel-writing subject expressed his/her estimation on the state of Peru as a whole and on its national character.

The majority of the travelers begin the narration of their trek through Peru, starting at Callao. This was primarily due to necessity, since Callao functioned as Lima's port city en route to Lima itself. Nevertheless, disembarking at Callao was an experience that was almost invariably commented on in a negative way. Lima, the famed Ciudad de los Reyes and administrative center for the viceroyalty of Peru during the period of Spanish colonialism, was a must-see for all the travelers examined.[9] The next city that was described and codified in detail was Arequipa.[10]

These cities, the major nodal points on an itinerary through Peru, are not necessarily important in themselves but rather important due to what rhetorical occasions they provided the travelers: what sites and sights the travelers take in while at these cities. Callao, Lima and Arequipa offered ample opportunities to examine and comment upon Peru's infrastructure and peoples. These cities also provided the occasion to analyze religious and cultural events—religious processions and celebrations as well as bullfights and cockfights. The journey to and from these cities also allowed travelers the occasion to represent the infrastructure and housing specific to the needs of the traveler: roadways and *tambos* (or inns), for example. These locales would manifest the raw data, the signs from which to discursively construct Peru as a "wretched" nation.

Landmarks and public gatherings, already highlighted through prescribed itineraries for their noteworthiness, were scrutinized for the possible application of certain key descriptors to attach to them. These descriptors are resonant of those used in colonial discourse and include most prevalently *filthy, superstitious, ignorant, indolent*—with the addition of *neglectful* and *disor-*

derly. Certain discourses that were used to justify the employment these descriptors comprised of the scientific discourses of miscegenation and social evolutionism; the historical discourse of the Black Legend; the religious discourse of Protestantism; and the political and philosophical discourses of liberalism and modernity.

Infrastructure and Structures: Places to See While in Peru
Let's look first at the travelers' occasions to speak about the state of Peru's landmarks, infrastructure and institutions. While at Callao, Lima and Arequipa, the traveler almost inevitably marks these places for their "poor" system of roads, sanitation and housing.

Lima most certainly was allotted the most textual space. It was the "famed" Ciudad de los Reyes that evoked a sense of great "dissapointment" upon entering the city. In certain sections of his *Diario* von Humboldt reports his disappointment in Lima after having heard that it was a magnificent city: "En Europa nos pintan a Lima como una ciudad de lujo, magnificencia ...Nada de todo eso he visto...No he visto ni casas muy adornadas ni señoras vestidas con demasiado lujo...En la noche, la inmundicia de las calles adornadas de perros y burros muertos, y la desigualdad del piso, impiden el correr en coche" (von Humboldt 86).[11] Von Humboldt's dissapointment suggests that his idea of Lima was based on the reports (or itineraries) of others. To register that disappointment, he focuses his attention on the *unadorned* housing as contrasted to the poor roadways *adorned* by *dead* burros—carrion in other words. The housing like the roads appear in a state of neglect and there seems to be no system of roadside sanitation in place. These sights at the site of Lima we will find to be conventional sights among the majority of the travelogues examined.

Darwin's description of Lima is strikingly similar to von Humboldt's in its focus and tone of disappointment. This is not surprising, however, since he cites von Humboldt in a footnote on the very page that Darwin offers the reader a negative representation of Lima: "The city of Lima is now in a wretched state of decay: the streets are nearly unpaved; and heaps of filth are piled up in all directions, where the black gallinazos, tame as poultry, pick up bits of carrion" (237).[12] This image of the turkey buzzard is as frequent in these texts as the renowned *tapada limeña*.[13] Among the travelers who include sightings of buzzards are Pfeifer (348); Brand (179; 49); Squire (461-462); Scherzer (78); Carleton (137); and Dahlgren (35-36).

This notion of disappointment is shared by Brand and Squire. Though Brand admits he spent less time in Peru than expected, he certainly found time to mention the carrion in the streets. "...I certainly cannot help expressing that I felt much disappointment, for it is, without exception, the dirtiest in South America—filth, dirt, and rubbish are to be seen in the streets all day long...until they are devoured by immense large birds, called turkey-buzzards, that are constantly to be seen devouring the various nuisances with which the streets are infested" (178-79). Squire explicitly warns other traveler's to temper their expectations when visiting Lima: "The traveller's first impressions of the place are not likely to be pleasing" (32). His disappointment stems from the architecture of the buildings ("painted fantastically" in patterns that remind one of a "checker-board" or a "barber's pole) and the "uneven" sidewalks and "rough" roads which are peopled by mounted donkey riders unmindful of passersby (32).

The male travelers are not the only ones that underscore the lack of a modern sewage system, system of roads or poor housing. Both Dahlgren and Tristan offer similar sights and negative commentaries on the matter (Dahlgren 35; Tristan 207). Likewise, the housing and roadways in both Callao and Arequipa fare no better in the texts of Scherzer and Darwin, who both underscore the degree of "filth" they find in those cities (Scherzer 73; Darwin 327).

The journey to and from these cities offers the traveler an opportunity to incorporate a discussion of Peru's *tambos*—which for the traveler are primitive and infested with fleas or rodents. The *tambo* becomes a sign at which housing and sanitation converge to indicate Peru's "lack" of reaching a modern state. For example, von Tschudi is quite dramatic in his estimation of the tambos: "One of these huts is a tambo, which can never be forgotten by any unfortunate traveller who may have taken up his abode in it...[W]oe to the unwary traveller who trusts himself in this dormitory! He soon finds himself surrounded by enemies from whose attacks it is impossible to escape; for the hut is infested with vermin" (von Tschudi 193). Squier characterizes Peruvian hospitality in terms of the lack of "universal" (expected by European and U.S. travelers) comforts found in Peru's tambos: "In Peru it [hospitality] consists generally in permitting you, with more or less of condescension, to spread your own bed on the mud floor of an unswept room, alive with vermin, with a single rickety table for its chief and often its only article of furniture" (247).[14]

Lima and Arequipa offer the traveler much to say about governmental and cultural buildings as well as the public programs they offer. As far as the buildings are concerned, if they are not "lacking" in maintenance (which indicates neglect), they are "lacking in good taste" (which indicates an ignorance in aesthetics according to an imperialist code of taste). Of the presidential palace in Lima, Pfieffer finds it unfit to be considered a palace: "The word palace is a very high-sounding title for such exceedingly shabby-looking buildings...they have rather a better appearance from the court-yards than from the outside. That of the President is particularly disfigured by a number of little booths that are plastered on to it" (344). Von Tschudi's estimation of it underscores a lack of [Western European] aesthetics: "On the north side of the square [Lima's Plaza Mayor] stands the government palace...The interior of the building corresponds with its outward appearance, being at once tasteless and mean" (52). The discussion of the museums and libraries—both represented as having a scarce number of specimens or books in the travelogues of von Tschudi and Pfeiffer eventually lead into discussions of Peru's educational system. On this topic, von Tschudi writes that, even at the better *colegios* which he's visited, "Professors, who themselves have never received any regular instruction, communicate their scanty share of knowledge in a very imperfect manner to the students" (90).[15]

Even though the travelogues examined here have varying publication dates that span a period of the 1820s to the 1880s, the sights elaborated are consistent among them. So, too, is the rhetoric used: each site and sight exudes neglect, filth, or poor taste to the degree that Peru has not advanced as a nation and remains in a state of "wretchedness."

The Curious Lab: People(s) to See (and Categorize) While in Peru

These principal cities also allow for the examination of Peruvian society and social organization. This examination takes place most frequently at the mention of religious gatherings and events of popular amusement. The representations of these public gatherings are inflected by the convergence of discourses such as Protestantism, miscegenation and the Black Legend. Having mentioned already the popularity of Prescott's *History* among travelers during the mid-late 1800s, a look at a passage from his work exposes how the anti-clericism or Protestantism, miscegenation and the Black Legend could blend together to constitute an *Other*.

The passages looked at concern the Spanish conquistador and colonizer as *Other*. Though Prescott admires the adventurous spirit of the Spanish conquistadors and religious, he is quick to point out their difference (both religious and racial) from the Anlgo-Saxon colonizers in the Northern hemisphere:

> Proud and vain-glorious...no danger could appall and no toil could tire him [the Spanish adventurer]....Yet in the motives of action...[h]is courage was sullied with cruelty, the cruelty that flowed equally—strange as it may seem—form his avarice and his religion...It was a convenient cloak for a multitude of sins... (Prescott 153)

Having pointed out the intersection of (Roman Catholic) religion with Spanish avarice, Prescott goes on to racialize the difference between the two colonizing powers:

> What a contrast did these children of Southern Europe present to the Anglo-Saxon races who scattered themselves along the great northern division of the Western hemisphere! For the principle of action with these latter was not avarice, nor the more specious pretext of proselytism; but independence—independence religious and political. (153)

Finally, the Spanish's decline in power is explained in terms of race, religion and lack of industriousness. Unlike the Protestant Anglo-Saxon colonizers who "were content with the slow but steady progress of their social polity," the Spanish colonizers were neither forced to employ a industrious work ethic, nor expend a great deal of self-determination to reap success. In effect the Spanish colonizers "of the neighboring continent, [shot] up into sudden splendors of a tropical vegetation, exhibited, even in their prime, the sure symptoms of decay" (154).

As for the downfall of the Inca empire, it fell due to the Inca people's "the Peruvians"—lack of understanding the "great law of human progress": "However industrious, he could not add a road to his own possessions…The great and universal motive to honest industry, that of bettering one's lot, was lost upon him. The great law of human progress was not for him" (64).

Imperialist travelers to Peru, whether predating or postdating the publication of Prescott's work, laden their representations of Peru's entire populous in a very similar rhetorical fashion. Many of the travelers convey a sense of amazement and disdain for the racial heterogeneity of Peru's population. For example, Pfeiffer offers a passage that is representative of most of the traveler's mention of the complex racial composition of Peru's inhabitants: "The inhabitants of Lima, like those of Acapulco, Callao, and I believe, all the Spanish-American States, are of such mixed Indian, European, and African blood, and proceed from such an inter-ramification of races, as can be found in no other quarter of the world" (Pfeiffer 349). Other travelers participate in descriptions of the racial diversity of the inhabitants—often underscoring character flaws associated with them (von Tschudi 64-74 and 80-81; Scherzer 88; Dahlgren 45; Darwin 327; Tristan 253-255).

But the mere inter-racial population is not solely at issue for the travelers. Rather the sharing of public space among the different races, classes and (to some degree) genders. Lines of demarcation and segregation are not clear or "orderly" as they were in their own countries, a situation that was often represented with a tone of frustration on the part of the travel-writer's effort to define their differences. Von Tschudi's texts is exemplary of this: "Possibly in no other place in the world is there so much variety of complexion and physiognomy as in Lima. From the delicately fair Creole daughter of the European parents, to the jet black Congo negro, people of every gradation of color are seen living in intimate relation one with another...to define their characteristics correctly would be impossible, for their minds partake of the mixture of their blood" (64-65).

The majority of the travelogues investigated inevitably include evaluative impressions upon having observed a religious procession or a mass, or upon viewing a bullfight or cockfight. In an age when naturalists influenced travel narratives and the urge to fit racial types into clearly delineated categories, the racial blurrings in Peruvian society and the audiences at religious celebrations and bull-fights which included all races, all classes, and both genders frustrated the writing subjects' taxonomic urge.

Religious gatherings generally allow for writers to comment on racial types and inject tones of anticlericism. For example, after attending mass in Lima, Dahlgren comments upon the inclusion of "the rude Indian" and "the Negro" among other types that not only attend mass but that have also influenced the Church to cater to them by decorating the interior of Lima's churches in order to encourage attendance (Dahlgren 42). When Tristan writes about the Passion play performed during Semana Santa in Arequipa, the notion of blurrings brings about a representation of "caos":

> Durante la Semana Santa...se da el Viernes Santo la representación del suplico de Jesús...Es la historia de la Pasión, sin omitir ninguna circunstancia, pero en vivo...*Una multitud confusa de hombres y mujeres de raza blanca, india y negra* sitian el calvario...El pueblo, los sacerdotes, la cruz, las ramas de olivo, todo mezclado, *forma un caos, un tumulto, una confusión espantosa...* (252; emphasis mine)

The passage just quoted is couched between commentaries that fault the Church for allowing such forms of celebration (Popular Catholicism) to denigrate the solemn reverence Tristan finds more appropriate. Before the passage, she writes that "La iglesia peruana explota en provecho de su influencia, el gusto de la población" (251). A few paragraphs after the passage, Tristan writes that these popular religious ceremonies takes away from the "esplendor" and "esterilidad" unlike one would find in Europe (252-253). Dahlgren and Tristan are not alone in relating their distaste of such celebrations and disapproval of how the religious interact with the masses; many other writers focus on events such as the one related by Tristan (Pfeiffer 344; Brand 189-191; von Tschudi 91).

Descriptions about bullfights generally allow in an element of the Black Legend (underscoring the inheritance of Spanish cruelty among the Peruvian love of the bullfight) and commentaries of surprise that women often attend these events. Von Tshudi, Brand and Dahlgren comment on the *limeñas'* delight at attending bullfights, which for each of these writers goes against Eurocentric notions of gender codes. For example, von Tschudi writes the following: "A mingled feeling of disgust and surprise takes possession of the European who witnesses the joy which pervades all classes of the inhabitants of Lima on the announcement of a bull-fight....They are barbarous diversions, and though they form a part of national customs, they are nevertheless a national disgrace" (109). Still von Tschudi tries to make some concessions for the Limeñas, writing that they've been trained since birth to enjoy such diversions.

The degree of regularity with which religious celebrations and bullfights as well as racial charts (in narrative descriptions rather than charts themselves) suggest prescribed sites and sights, in turn indicating to the reader that these comprise some of the conventions common in nineteenth-century travelogues about Peru. Likewise, elaboration on poor housing, roadways, and the lack of sanitation system inundate travelogues such of these point to other sites and sights, must-sees to include. Yet, the occasion to attend these sites and include observations that are repeated with a great deal of regularity, is not born solely out of curiosity.

Itineraries were not followed solely for authorial purposes of conforming to the genre as it pertained to Peru to build authority. Rather the sights made possible through adhering to these itineraries fed representational modes intended to "prove" the Peruvian *Other(s)* was/were, indeed, inferior. A presupposition that Peru was a backward nation in need of the guiding influence the imperialist nations could provide, was already in place through imperialist desire and subsequent agendas. Desire fed the agendas and agendas needed to mask themselves through the *Other* to legitimate foreign presence in Peru for the economic betterment of imperialist nations. This underscores the ideologically-charged nature of travelers' narratives about Peru—the driving force behind processing what the writing subject saw in a manner that would explain Peru's failure to reach a modern, competitive and progressive state.

That failure was due rhetorically to an *inferior national character*. Bullfights are representative as national customs, indicative of national disgrace (von Tschudi 14); turkey buzzards are touted as national birds (Dahlgren 36); unkempt interiors of Peruvian homes become "typical of the national character" (von Tschudi 73); the intermingling among races and classes of Peruvian people(s) become national obstacles in the way of Peru's pathway to Progress

(Dahlgren 42). No other traveler suggests this as clearly as Sherzer does. According to him, Peru needs the Anglo-Saxon expertise to cure it of its pre-Modern ills. For Scherzer, only a Nordic wave of immigration can ameliorate Peru's situation, since its *mestizo* population is a race prone to "la holgazaneería y torpeza":

> Sean norteamericanos, ingleses o alemanes, siempre serán los descendientes de una raza más enérgica, los que transformen aquí el carácter de la raza meridional, que despierten con una nueva mente espiritual....Solamente una gran emigración nórdica puede dar impuso a estos países [como el del Perú], comercial y políticamente, explotar y aprovechar sus abundantes riquezas naturales y asegurarles una digna posición entre los estados civilizados del mundo. (102-03)

With conventional representations such as these, one understands the urgency with which Peruvian travel-writers offered contestatory representations on their own nation in an effort to secure its place as an autonomous nation.

Notes

1. What people often refer to and read as Columbus' journal (his *Diario*) comes from Bartólome de Las Casas' edition of the journal, supplemented by Casas' own commentary (Zamora 199). However, since Las Casas includes direct quotes from Columbus and offsets them from Las Casas' own commentary as a editorial subject, what lines I examine from the Diario are what Zamora considers to be examples of "direct citation [with] the repetition of the first-person pronoun" purported to be the Admiral's own words—"set in relief against the background of the indirect discourse..." (Zamora 55).

2. See also Spurr's chapter on surveillance in his *The Rhetoric of Empire*. Both Spurr and Pratt build upon Michel Foucault's discussion of the panopticon and apply it to travel writing because the power that the travel writing subject exerts through his/her authoritative surveying gaze acts similarly to that of the supervisor's controlling gaze over the inmates through the panopticon tower of a prison. See section, "Panopticism," in *Discipline and Punish* (Foucault 200-209).

3. In fact, Mrs. Howard Vincent's *From China to Peru* makes reference to the writings of Columbus (267).

4. Michael Adas comments that the Western European philosophers of the 1700s, such as Voltaire, were influenced by the work of Buffon and Bacon, viewed America as immature, and its peoples, like its surroundings, were stunted physically and easily subjugated by nature (77). For example, Voltaire writes in his Essai sur les moeurs (1765) that "[t]here is one observation to be made on the nations of the New World...namely that the peoples that live further away from the tropics have always been invincible, and those nearest the tropics have almost always been submitted to monarchs..." (42).

5. For example, Prescott implores his readers to follow the trek to the areas of the Inca like von Humboldt had. In doing so, he directly quotes von Humboldt: "Every scholar will agree with Humboldt in the wish that 'some learned traveller would visit the borders of the lake of Titicaca, the district of Callao, and the high plains of Tiahuancaco, the theater of the ancient American civilization'" (Prescott 34).

6. For this group of "yungas" that he is describing, he is concentrating on those peoples populating the region between Jauja and Ica.

7. Later in this chapter, we will find that nineteenth-century travel writers to Peru repeat the characterization of Peruvians as being indolent and extravagant with drink. In the case of the imperialist travel writers, however, the term indolence applies to all Peruvians, no longer to just the indigenous peoples of Peru.

8. Lest one be surprised that Garcilaso and his writings should be well-received given that he was mestizo, Stuart Schwartz reminds us that, what he terms, a first-generation mestizo who was born of two noble lineages—for example, the son of a Spanish father of nobility and a mother of Indian royalty—allowed for a certain degree of acceptance. A first-generation

mestizo could be afforded a status that could forego the stigma of mestizo which proceeding generations of mestizos generally suffered (Schwartz 187). Garcilaso, thus, serves as a prime example of this, and Garcilaso was quick to point out that he was son of a noble Spaniard and of royal Inca mother.

9. Originally the Black Legend emanated from the Spanish friar, Bartolomé de Las Casas' *Brevísima relación de la destrución de Las Indias* (1552). In it Las Casas recounted and criticized the abuses and brutality commited against the indigenous peoples by the Spanish conquistadores and colonizers. Due to its rapid translation into French, English, German, Italian and Dutch and due to its enormous circulation and dissemination, it became a text manipulated and used to malign Spain's "right" to control its Spanish American colonies and barring its colonies from trading with other European world powers (Chang-Rodríguez and Filer 28-29). Deborah Poole explains how the Black Legend was appropriated later by the French during the Enlightenment: "Although written as part of a specific debate concerning the role of religion and the Church in the Spanish conquest of the New World, Las Casas's text was taken up by the philosophes [of the French Enlightenment] as proof of the irrationality and fanaticism that had corrupted Iberian society in general and the Catholic Church in particular" (Poole 36). However, the travelogues gathered for the purposes of this book suggest that German, U.S., and British travel-writers of the nineteenth century appropriated it in much the same way as the French did during the Enlightenment.

10. For a list of the corpus of travelogues, please see the bibliography under the listings of "Core" and "Secondary" primary texts.

11. Two other cities frequented by the travelers were Cuzco and, to a lesser degree, Puno. Cuzco and Puno were generally included if the traveler was interested in Inca structures—either as a researcher in the field like von Tschudi, Squire and Markham or as an amateur enthusiast such as in the case of De Sartiges.

12. In regards to von Humboldt's impressions of Lima, his "Diario" is of great importance as Manuel Vegas Vélez points out. The importance of it lies in the fact that much of Humbodlt's writings that have been published—among them *Viaje a las Regiones Equinocciales*; *Cuadros de Naturaleza* (1876) and *Cosmos* (1876)—fail to include his impressions of Lima. Therefore, his "Diario," is an important work to consider in this regard. Though portions of his diary were published in German approximately during the period of 1815-1832, the German publication failed to include journal entries regarding Peru specifically. Later in 1986 a complete translation came out first in French, then, in German by Margot Faak. In 1991 Manuel Vegas Vélez translated into Spanish Humboldt's journal entries that pertain to his travels through Peru specifically: *Humboldt en el Perú*.

13. Besides Darwin's reference to von Humboldt's work, he also cites von Tschudi. Von Tschudi also emphasizes the poor state of the roads upon entering Lima from Asamayo and Chancay, writing that"[t]he roads are very wearisome both to horse and rider, especially in the declivities towards the plains" (159). Moving onward from Chancay and closer to Lima, the roads are minimally improved since "[f]rom thence the road runs through a stony tract, partially strewn with the large masses of rock, called the Piedras gordas" (159).

Von Tschudi's comment on the interior of Lima's houses also indicate neglect. He likens the interior of houses in Lima to "stables" lacking in cleanliness—which he finds indicative ("typical") of Peru's "national character" (73).

14. Because the topic of the tapada is such an important convention, a detailed analysis of how representations of her change under proto-feminist, nationalist and imperialist agendas, a large section of chapter two is dedicated to the tapada.

15. He characterizes another tambo in the same manner. See pages 252-253.

16. For similar commentaries, see also De Sartiges (12-13) and Pfeiffer (347).

• CHAPTER THREE •

Constructing Peru: Imperialist Representations of a "Backward" Nation

In Mary Schriber's study of American travel writers of the nineteenth and early twentieth century, she notes that women and men shared itineraries and attitudes in their consideration of the host cultures that they traveled to (Schriber 61). As we shall see in this chapter, men and women travelers to nineteenth-century Peru shared similar discourses as well. The one commonality that brings these travel writers together regardless of their country of origin or their gender is that each one is engaged in the constant process of trying to authorize him/herself as a writing subject saturated by a "civilizing worth" to help further Peru on its linear path toward Progress. As regards the travelogues under consideration, some discourses underwent little modification by the female writing subjects, while other discourses did undergo certain iterative shifts in the repetition of certain discourses.

All of the texts under examination for this chapter, for the most part, relate to Pratt's designation of travelogues that exhibit a capitalist vanguard ideology. This chapter will center around the following travel narratives: Madeleine Vinton Dahlgren's *South Sea Sketches* (1881); Flora Tristan's *Peregrinaciones de una paria* (1838); and J.J. von Tschudi's *Travels in Peru, during the Years 1838-1842* (1847).[1] Tristan is included as a special case, however, because, due to her proto-socialist tone, she doesn't completely fit the category of capitalist vanguardist. In fact, according to Pratt, women writers of the period, Tristan included, in her study are instead better categorized in a category all their own: as social exploratresses, women travelers who manipulate their travelogues to voice their critiques for social reform (160).

However, bracketing off the women writers from their male counterparts suggests too complete a division and, thus, mutes the extent to which the women writers endorse or at least reinforce the imperialist agendas of their nations. Women travel writers such as Dahlgren and Tristan can't be left in a category that solely focuses on their quality as female-gendered social reformers alone without also examining in a more detailed manner how they are very much complicit in reinforcing the imperialist project either wittingly so (as in the case of Dahlgren) or unwittingly so. They are duplicitous in assuming a position of "superiority" in contrast to the Peruvians they write about not only due to their country of origin or class position but equally due to their race. On this point I agree with Elizabeth Spellman's urging that we not bypass issues of race because "...attempts to focus on gender in isolation from other aspects of identity such as race and class can work to obscure the effect race, class, and gender have on each other" (Spellman 114). For this reason, I will include a two-fold analysis of the women writers. I will first look at both men and women travel writers from Europe and North America as a group sharing a position of imperial ethos, a sense of "superiority" that condones imperial intervention into the politics and culture of "lesser" nations. Then, I will examine how the female subjects incorporate special traits to keep in mind: how women inject gender into their narratives and how they negotiate their inclusion of political critique and commentary regarding both Peru and their own country of origin.

This chapter is organized according to a two-fold examination of tropes of subject-authorization. The first part will look at how each subject participates in tropes of "othering" to place him/herself at a higher rung in the hierarchy of "civilized" subject. These tropes involve inferiorizing certain Peruvians according to race, region, and manners. We will look at the similarities among both the women as well as the men complicit in ascribing to an ethos of superiority over their foreign or even national "others." The second part of the chapter, however, looks at how female travel-subjects depart from their male contemporaries in overtly "feminine" rhetorical strategies. As Schriber has pointed out in her own study of U.S. women's travelogues regarding their travels abroad, women do "inject" (that is to say they textually emphasize) their gender difference into their works in explicit and implicit ways. As regards the female subjects, this two-part examination is intended to shed light on the constant oscillation between using traditional imperialist discourses (seemingly universal and, therefore, hiding the male genderedness implicit in the discourses) and employing blatantly female-gendered representations.

First, what discursive traits do men and women share in their travelogues in their push to authorize a North American or Western European "guiding" presence in Peru? Common to all of the texts are the subjects' highlighting of what are considered to be signs of Peru's splendor: Peru's natural resources and the ruins and monuments that testify to Inca civilization. These two types of evidence of Peru's splendor serve two discursive purposes, the first being that they provide sufficient interest for the reader on a content level. The second purpose, whether wittingly or unwittingly incorporated, is to paint Peru as an alluring destination for the prospective traveler, resident, reformer and/or investor.

Upon underscoring Peru's abundant natural resources many of the travelers studied here provide an informal inventory. Two resources that receive attention in these travel narratives concern the guano reserves on the Chinca islands or the rich Peruvian soil and its potential for a high yield of European crops. Von Tschudi includes commentary on both; however, his gaze seems much more attuned to the rich possibilities for introducing and harvesting European crops from the Peruvian landscape.

Von Tschudi dedicates his seventh chapter to the geography of Peru and Peru's cultivation practices and crop yields. He first comments on the crops popular with Peruvians before presenting a discussion on what European crops he thinks would be suitable and successful if planted in the various regions of Peru. After finishing his inventory of Peruvian foodstuffs (cotton, sugar cane, maize, potatoes and beans), von Tschudi positions his gaze in the future tense, ripe with a notably Eurocentric hunger and desire. For example he writes that "[a]ll vegetables of the cabbage and salad kinds cultivated in Europe will grow in Peru. The climate, both of the coast and of the hills, suits them perfectly" (127). This future tense makes it obvious that the traveler's discourse here is not innocent but rather brings his nation's agenda and its future well-being with him whether consciously or not.

Once von Tschudi has exhausted his commentary on vegetable crops, he moves on to the bounty of fruit and how abundantly it thrives in certain agricultural sectors of Peru. In the following quote, one notes paradise entering von Tschudi's diction through his use of words like "luxuriantly," "perfection" and "abundance": "All the fruits of southern Europe thrive luxuriantly in the warm regions of Peru...Though the trees bloom and bear fruit the whole year round, yet there are particular times in which their produce is in the greatest perfection and abundance" (130).

Von Tschudi is specific with his inventory of European crops whether currently successful or pinpointed for future planting. He underscores for future European farmers where best to plant their crops: plant European grains in the interior (130); European fruit trees in the Sierra (130); and European salad vegetables in the coastal regions (127). Peru's soil becomes mapped with European intention. Discursive power takes root like seeds planted beneath the surface to prepare the way for European expertise (and subsequent exploitation) to insert itself into Peru's "well-being."

Although von Tschudi insists that the Peruvian soil is fertile and ripe with potential, he admits a certain downfall naturalized as an "inherent" Peruvian flaw of neglect and incompetence. For von Tschudi, the Peruvians' agricultural prowess lacks "superior" European industriousness and profitable crop management. It is not enough that Europeans have sent their seeds to

Peruvian farmers; the European agrarian's presence, skill and fortitude are "necessary" for success. On this point, von Tschudi writes: "The praiseworthy attempts made by many Europeans, who have sent seeds and young plants to Peru, have failed of success, owing to the indifference of the natives to the advancement of those objects" (130).

Dahlgren's inventory of the landscape and the fertile or infertile possibilities that lie there in is concise as a brief comment here and there but nothing that extends beyond the length of a paragraph. However, she undoubtedly also keeps an eye out for exposing which areas are more fertile than others. On her way from Callao to Lima, one finds a very quick inventory of the more fertile regions:

> On the sierras, or high tablelands of Peru, lie many fertile valleys; but the low lands are sandy, and as no rain falls, they are sterile, unless irrigated. In the lower portion of Peru say from 5° to 15° rain never falls, although heavy dews serve to support vegetation…The small river Rimac encircles the valley…and, debauching into the sea at Callao, irrigates and fertilizes the country around. (Dahlgren 23)

Though the women writers are not as detailed in their inventories, they do, indeed, include comments that would appeal to foreign investors. Dahlgren is especially exemplary on this point when she includes an account of her visiting the Chinca islands and notes the rich possibility surrounding their guano reserves:

> These three small islands make a desolate group to the eye, although the source of vast wealth to Peru, and forming indeed her principal revenue. One of the three has been nearly stripped of its deposits…but it is said that the remaining two will not prove so productive; although immense quantities cover their cragged rocks… (104)

Though Dahlgren originally points out that the wealth belongs to Peru, she offers anecdotal evidence that the wealth is accessible to foreign investors as well, commenting on a rich "monopolist" from Newport "whose enormous fortune was made in this traffic" (104). This is particularly indicative of foreign investment and exploitation already taking place regarding Peru's guano market.

Dahlgren even goes so far as to scold her own nation for not taking a more active role in its commerce with Peru, considering this to be a "national humiliation" for the U.S., since European nations like England have the upper-hand in the area: "It is extremely mortifying to a patriotic American that we have, so to speak, no commerce; and if we had [,] we never could compete with this free-trade from Europe" (34). Later in the text she again takes up the topic and laments over her nation's "humiliation": "England has acquired sway in the South Seas...and at every step we are reminded of our country's unfortunate loss of commerce" (103).

Whereas the male writers spend more textual space on the specific natural resources, the women provide anecdotal evidence of the potential wealth awaiting their compatriot businessmen and entrepreneurs to take advantage of markets and professions not yet flooded by Peruvian merchants and professionals. Dahlgren, after providing an example of an "enormously rich" American who made his wealth by "getting a contract to supply the country with ice," assures the reader that this example should not be considered an isolated case: "This is but one instance, for large fortunes are made here by enterprising business men" (62-63). A chapter later Dahlgren provides another example of the potential wealth to be reaped by her countrymen. She recounts a conversation she had with an American dentist in Callao known as "the principal dentist of the country" who assures Dahlgren (and the reader by extension) that he is "making money fast" (83).

Though one encounters this call to compatriot businessmen less frequently in Tristan's text, she does, indeed, mention that France did not take full advantage of cornering several markets for exporting French products to Peru such as wine:

> Cuando el gobierno francés reconoció la independencia de los Estados de la América Española, se hizo gran ruido en los periódicos de París, sobre los cónsules enviados por el ministerio. Éstos iban...a abrir nuevos mercados para nuestros productos...Hubiera sido fácil a esos cónsules aprovechar del odio de la América del Sur contra su antiguas metrópolis española y portuguesa, para hacer admitir los vinos de Francia con derechos menores que los impuestos a los vinos de la Península. (195-196)

Keeping in mind these women's comments and their somewhat tempered chastisement of their countries' commerce policies with Peru, it becomes clear that there was a real global competition taking place, a race to tap into certain commercial endeavors implanted on and secured from Peru's landscape. Though von Tschudi does not criticize his nation's negotiating abilities in this area, he is, nevertheless, quick to note that the German presence in Peru is much less than that of the U.S., England or France (85).

In addition to pointing out the splendid potential of Peruvian natural resources, these writing subjects also accentuate whenever possible discussions of Inca civilization inspired by their visits to ruins or their travels along routes via Inca-constructed roadways. Mention of Inca ruins as breathtaking testaments to Inca ingenuity and grandeur is clearly a convention in travel writing about Peru; however, description and detail of them, in the case of North American and European travelogues, is not as lengthy as those passages that linger on the topic of Peru's "poor" administration and infrastructure and its "uncouth" population. This disproportionate textual space given to all the "flaws" noted in Peruvian culture according to the foreign traveler hints toward the symbolic inclusion of Inca ruins: they serve as indicators of possible greatness achievable in Peru only if it hosts the appropriate "guiding" and "civilizing" presence, then, lacking at the time (in the minds of the foreign travelers).

Once generating interest to the site of Peru, the issue becomes how to warrant the need for a call to action to civilize the region according to a European or North American model. The discursive answer is to freeze Peru into a backward time; Peru becomes anachronistic in the modern world. This technique of freezing Peru into a backward, premodern time relates to what Fabian has termed a denial of "coeval" time. Denial of coeval time involves discursive instances in which the traveler represents him/herself as living in the present modern time, whereas the objects of his/her discourse inhabit a premodern time (Fabian 31).

There are four primary areas we to consider, each of which "attests" to a backward Peruvian nation due to its a) poor infrastructure; b) poor administration; c) poor aesthetics; and d) racial diversity.

The Inca sites become markers of contrast always pointing toward the "wretchedness" surrounding them. In his travels southward of Lima, when von Tschudi comes across some monuments and ruins near Chilca, he presents the reader with the notorious division—the wealth of an Inca past split off from the time of Peru's forlorn present: "...here and there the scattered monuments of the wealth and greatness of bygone ages present a remarkable and painful contrast to present poverty and misery..." (von Tschudi160). In a similar vein Dahlgren writes: "Peru has to this day the benefit of the splendid roads built by the Incas...Indeed, vestiges everywhere abound of a former superior cultivation of the soil, and of a far greater populousness than at present" (24; my emphasis).

All the European and North American travelogues under consideration for the purposes of this study make their judgement clear as to who is responsible for the country's demise: it is Peru's own neglect that produced the sordid state of affairs of national proportion. Neglect and Progress form two ends of the positivist spectrum, and the North American and European travelers, men and women alike, constantly employ the contrast of the two. As Pratt points out, "neglect became the touchstone of a negative esthetic that legitimated European interventionism" (149).

The travelers construct the spectrum as a way to calibrate the state of Peruvian civilization: at the one end, the remnants of Inca empire; at the other, Peru's national failure to modernize and attain Progress as defined by imperial powers. Each end of the spectrum is clearly metaphoric. Alison Blunt sees travel as a great producer of metaphor as the traveler constructs meaning in his/her text: "By definition, metaphor is inherently spatial in that it connects two seemingly disconnected ideas in order to construct meaning" (Blunt 15). In the positivist spectrum that the North American and European travel writers proffer, the Inca ruins and Peruvian soil make apparent attainable wealth in the region already proven by the Incan empire. The other end of the spectrum invites a "civilizing presence" to ameliorate the apparent moral and industrial abandonment of the Peruvian government. One end garners interest; the other end sanctions action.

A principal way to condemn Peru's administration is to obsess textually over the poor infrastructure and administration policies of the nation whether regarding the physical upkeep of the roads, housing and institutions or the education and moral character of the people. Focusing primarily on the citadel of Santa Catalina and its barracks, von Tschudi, in one broad representational stroke takes this example of a governmental building to represent public buildings in aggregate: "They are remarkable for want of cleanliness, and like most of the public buildings in this interesting city going fast to decay" (von Tschudi 62).

Likewise, depopulation points toward a degraded state of Peruvian "reality." David Spurr asserts that "colonial discourse takes over as it takes cover," describing the process of the colonizer appropriating the colonized land as his own while simultaneously effacing that very appropriation under the guise of the colonized plea for help in managing the territory (Spurr 28). This plea then takes on the form of a "putative appeal" which, according to Spurr, might guise itself as "absence that calls for affirming presence," especially in a region ripe with monetary potential (28). Von Tschudi paints a sad scene of towns losing their population, which exemplifies the rhetorical use of absence to suggest the need of "guidance." After discussing different demographic studies that give varying figures as to whether or not Lima is suffering from a decline in population, von Tschudi sets out to prove that such is the case: "This [the waning in population] is sufficiently proved by the fact that several parts of the city are now totally uninhabited: the houses falling to decay, and the gardens lying in waste" (von Tschudi 63).

For von Tschudi declines in population and decaying or unkempt structures are physical signifiers that indicate, in an abstract manner, the moral character of the nation. Von Tschudi connects poor housing with poor national character: the decaying houses and unkempt gardens and uninhabited homes are "easily explained by the physical and political condition of the country" (63). Even the interior of homes implicates Peru by extension:

> In the interior of the houses cleanliness does not extend beyond those apartments which are open to visitors...The other rooms of the house frequently bear more resemblance to a stable...But, even this is typical of the national character, a great outward show and little inward worth. (73; my emphasis)

Von Tschudi views management as the key signifier of Progress. He is clear on this point when he describes the condition and management of Peru's hospitals, libraries and museums. Regarding the National Museum in Lima, von Tschudi infantilizes Peru's location on the timeline of Progress: "As yet the establishment is quite in its infancy. It contains nothing of scientific value...it would differ but little from the collections of curiosities frequently formed by amateurs, in which all sorts of heterogeneous objects are jumbled together" (58). The message behind the previous quote is analogous: the whole of Peru like its national museum needs order. Peru has not only failed to modernize it has failed in the basic upkeep of structures already in place.

Whereas von Tschudi focuses his contempt more on the decay of structures and poor management of institutions, other writers who traveled through Peru such as Brand and Carleton, emphasize the "filth" they find in Peruvian towns and cities. Regarding his observations of Lima, Charles Brand expresses his disappointment in Lima: "...I certainly cannot help expressing that I felt much disappointment, for it is, without exception, the dirtiest in South America filth, dirt, and rubbish are to be seen in the streets all day long..." (Brand178). Brand (179), Carleton (137) and Dahlgren (35-36) fix their gaze on the turkey-buzzard (gallinazo o buitre) as proof of not only the extent of the rubbish in Lima, but also the neglect of the government to provide public sanitation and trash removal. Dahlgren even proposes to appoint the turkey-buzzard as the national symbol of Peru: "Flocks of ungainly turkey-buzzards brood over these dirty gutters, where all garbage is thrown. These birds act, in great part, as scavengers for the city...If ubiquity, utility, and enduring vitality can entitle them to such a preeminence, they may fairly be called the national bird" (35-36).

As the reader will observe from the quote above, the women travelers share in this same lamentation and disgust for the ragged state of Peru's infrastructure. Revisiting the following quote from Dahlgren, one finds that Dahlgren also splits time into an ingenious Inca past contrasted to a present backwardness. "Peru has to this day the benefit of the splendid roads built by the Incas...Indeed, vestiges everywhere abound of a former superior cultivation of the soil, and of a far greater populousness than at present" (24). Dahlgren's quote is especially useful in showing the transitional turn from the splendid past to the forlorn present. Though her quote admires the Inca roads for the splendid ingenuity they signify, what once signified ingenuity now becomes reminders of Peru's lack of modernization again furthering the split between a splendid bygone age that tantalizes the archeological interest of readers and the "backward" and "wretched" state of the nation's present infrastructure that "begs" for intervention.

Much like von Tschudi, Dahlgren constantly points out "forlorn" and "wretched" housing everywhere in Islay (106); in Iquique (110) as well as what she finds to be "desolate" land, neglected by "proper" methods of cultivation, especially at the Chinca islands where there is an alluring reserve of guano (104). If Dahlgren fails to condemn the housing in the more metropolitan areas of Peru, Tristan does not. Of the housing in Lima Tristan writes: "Cómo no encontré nada que mereciera la atención, subí a la torre para ver la ciudad a vuelo de pájaro. Esta soberbia ciudad tiene el aspecto más miserable, cuando la vista se detiene en ella. Sus casas descubiertas hacen en efecto de ruinas" (207).

For all of the travel writers considered here there is a definite linkage between signifiers of poor administration, poor infrastructure, and, perhaps, more damning, poor aesthetics. The topic of "bad taste" echoes throughout these travelogues. Just as imperialist discourse constructs a need for European and North American cultivation of Peru's soil, as von Tschudi points out, so, too, does it build a need for the cultivation of Peru's taste. When describing the procession that takes place during the Fiesta de Santa Rosa, Dahlgren connects a nation's sense of aesthetics as an indicator of its progress:

> That which makes the gross materialism of the spectacle [of the barbaric taste of the masses] is purely the outcropping of the rude taste of a semi-civilized people. Yet the idea which stirs them is divine, is spiritual; and we join in the common aspiration." (Dahlgren 80-81)

After deploring the "unrefined taste" with which the celebrants exhibit, Dahlgren writes that a fusion of divine idea and cultured exhibition will take place with time and progress: "When the time shall come that these races shall be educated to a clearer perception of the aesthetic, we will then have purer representations of this   ideal principle. (81)

According to Tristan, there are "crude" church relics (247), mirrors in houses that lack "taste" (249) and "primitive" cuisine (249). Even Peru's most promising museums lack funding due to the society's lack of taste. For Tristan, "[e]l gusto por las bellas artes sólo se manifiesta en la edad avanzada de las naciones"—and in her estimation and representation, Peru has not reached such a state of advancement (209).

One should note that in the quotes just seen taken from both Tristan and Dahlgren's texts, both are anti-clerical up to a point. Each of them qualify the anti-clerical tone as a charge against popular Catholicism, or what Tristan labels Peruvian Catholicism: "La iglesia peruana explota en provecho de su influencia, el gusto de la población" (251). In describing a mass that she attends, Tristan writes, "En Europa las bellas artes cubren...con un brillante barniz la insípida esterilidad de las ceremonias. Por lo demás, en el Perú, no se frecuentan las iglesias sino como sitios de reunión. El grado de civilización alcanzado por un pueblo se refleja en todo" (253). Again we see the progressivist discourse with its focus on calibrating civilization linearly, the standard for aesthetics being clearly a Eurocentric one.

For Tristan, her dislike of the popular or "Peruvian Catholicism" is twofold: 1) it serves to exploit what Tristan considers the "incredulous" nature of the masses; and 2) it leaves them uneducated and without taste. For Dahlgren, the disgust she reserves for popular Catholicism is that it reinforces and symbolically condones the "savage taste" of the races she feels best exemplify the masses, the "rude Indian" and the "Negro." Upon describing the interiors of the churches of Lima, Dahlgren writes disapprovingly: "Great wealth, without the guidance of good taste, has been here lavished. They tell us that this sacrifice of the purer rules of art has often been made in order to better adapt devotion to the rude Indian. We cannot but deplore such a mistake, and feel that the savage taste ought to be raised to the proper ideal standard, not the standard lowered to suit the untutored mind" (41).

A trait common to all of the European and North American travelers under consideration is to paint Peru as a nation "burdened" by the multitude of races. In fact, racial mapping whether in the form of charts or of narrative descriptions of the variety of peoples found in South America was a well-established convention in travelogues of the period. One should not be surprised then to find that each of the travel writers under study engage in one way or another in this practice.[2]

Von Tschudi writes with a tone of amazement upon viewing that racial diversity that Peru presents:

> Possibly in no other place in the world is there so much variety of complexion and physiognomy as in Lima. From the delicately fair Creole daughter of European parents, to the jet black Congo Negro, people of every gradation of color are seen living in intimate relation one with another. (64)

Von Tschudi, in this introductory comment that occurs before his detailed racial map, makes the two most identifiable races clear and his choice of adjectives registers for the reader which of the races is superior: the "delicately fair Creole" is no doubt closest to the archetypal European signifier of "classic" beauty of Woman—"delicately fair" as opposed to the "jet black." The racial mapping and its complexity emphasize another area of burden and obstacle to Peru's progress. However, the more von Tschudi tries to control the varying object of his gaze, the Peruvian in every "gradation," the more he encounters difficulty in properly identifying and classifying each and every race. In trying to define the mixed races, von Tschudi admits that "[u]nlike the two extreme classes—the whites and blacks—...to define their characteristics correctly would be impossible, for their minds partake of the mixture of their blood" (65).

Miscegenation disturbs the dichotomy of black/white; it challenges the power of the gaze because gaging the amount of mixture eludes the eye. Mixed races remain untamable because they defy the classificatory cages the Anglo travelers would place them in. As David Cahill has noted the nature of socio-racial categories was "protean" throughout Peru's history, thanks to an already complex system of kinship in place in pre-incaic times made more complex by the Spaniards' "obsession with limpieza de sangre, caste and status" (345).

The fact of the close proximity and interaction between the races seems equally disturbing to von Tschudi. The "burden" of Peru's racial diversity seems to be, in fact, greater for the white European and North American who finds his/her efforts to classify the races constantly frustrated by subtle changes in skin tone; hence the need to focus on taste and manners and customs as signifiers of non-white Peruvians especially at public festivals examined later.

This multiplication of races overlaps into an additional burden of a complexly stratified system of classes complicated, furthermore (according to the travelers' mode of thinking) the racial blurring that miscegenation produces. The following quote from *South Sea Sketches* points out this constructed connection best: "But the real trouble in Peru, which would indeed seem to forbid any rapid change for the better, consists in the great variety of races, and in the degraded state of the various classes" (Dahlgren 45).

In the above-mentioned quote, one notices that class and race are not altogether distant categories but, in fact, often come into play with one another when estimating the national culture of Peru as a whole. This dual mention of class and race occurs in the description of the "Negro" women participating in the Fiesta of Santa Rosa St. Rose being the patron saint of Lima. Dahlgren first fusses about the Negro women's "flimsy" attire, "tricked out" with adorning roses and their "swaying" movements; then, she associates it with the "tastelessness," seemingly exemplified by the Negro women, who signify on a more general level the whole of the masses:

> We get a glimpse of a number of shabby-looking peasants, and we are satisfied if not gratified. Negro women, draped in the flimsiest gauze ball dresses, and tricked out with pink roses stuck in their wool, burn incense with a swaying movement. All this helps to give a fuller idea of the barbaric taste of the masses, to which the clergy seems to defer on such occasions. (80)

One finds from the above-mentioned quote, Dahlgren finishes her commentary, which first started out as clearly racist, with a classist summation of the lack of aesthetics.

Like Dahlgren, Tristan's measuring gaze of civilization and the lack thereof obsesses over the negro and sambo participants in the procession Nuestra Santa in Arequipa. Tristan's penchant for freezing Peru into an anachronistic time intersects with the object of her gaze, the Afro-Peruvians hired by the church as dancers and musicians. By the tone and diction that accompanies Tristan's ethnographic gaze, it becomes obvious that the Afro-Peruvian characters serve as indicators of uncivilization. She does not describe them simply as dancing, but rather "hacían gestos y contorsiones de una cínica desvergüenza, molestaban a las negras y muchachas de color...les dirigían toda clase de frases obscenas...Era una confusión grotesca en donde se oían gritos y risas convulsas y aparté los ojos con disgusto" (Tristan 213). For Tristan, like the procession in Arequipa just described, Lima, too, offers the same canivalesque processions, though, in Tristan's estimation, they are "aun más cómicas y indecentes que las que tanto me escandalizaron en Arequipa" (225). The participants in these processions (the only ones her gaze seems to take in for the more lengthy descriptions) are those she finds most representative of "scandal" and "indecency": the negros and sambos.

Tristan's gaze conveniently excludes the fact that these festivals found a plethora of actors of diverse racial identity. When Tristan does mention that Caucasian people can also be found in these celebrations, she is very brief, only including them in a phrase lacking the same vivid fervor of the passage previously mentioned. She writes flatly that during Holy Week one could find "una multitud de hombres y mujeres de raza blanca, india y negra" (252). In the case of these women travel writers both represent the black inhabitants as caricatures; these women writers are complicit in adopting a very imperialist discourse that clings to racism to prove the wretchedness and backwards nature of nations that need the "civilizing" presence of white, middle and upper-class Europeans and Euro-Americans. These women are able to elevate their status to that of the authorized imperial subject whose gaze sets in to classify and evaluate all that it surveys. In this way, Tristan and Dahlgren exhibit what scholars like Blunt and Mills have noted in other white bourgeois traveling women from imperial nations: they "became increasingly able to share in the authority of male colonizers" because "racial status constructed by colonial discourses of difference overcame the gender inferiority created by patriarchal discourses of difference" (Blunt 36). Smith adds that even the spatial distance from their home societies further "disemburdens" women travel writers because "at the margins of the empire, far from the European center's hold, they could as white women break through the borderland and of female embodiment and achieve a mobility of autobiographical script unavailable to them in the 'home' country" (Smith 413).

This is not to say that Tristan and Dahlgren weren't sensitive to the inequality and brutality suffered by slaves. Both women condemned slavery. For example, in the case of Tristan, after a long racializing and racist description of an African man whose dress exemplified his backwardness, Tristan included a conversation she had with a slave trader and notes to the reader through her dialogue with a co-passenger, her disgust for the man and his business: "Debía usted ver en la expresión de mi rostro que este hombre me inspira la más profunda repugnancia" (Tristan 75). Tristan later refers to slavery as "el monstruoso ultraje a la humanidad: la esclavitud" (80). Interestingly, in the very same chapter that Dahlgren carnavalizes the Afro-Peruvian women participants at the Fiesta de Santa Rosa, Dahlgren applauds both U.S. President Abraham Lincoln and Peru's "patriot Castillas" as being great "empancipator[s] of a race in servitude" (85).

It is interesting to speculate, however, about the placement of these abolitionist statements mentioned above. Both those of Tristan and those of Dahlgren appear in the exact same chapters where black caricatures abound earlier. One wonders: do these textual instances of anti-slavery assertions which occur soon after caricaturized portraits of black inhabitants point to any anxiety on the part of the writing subject that the trope of "othering" is unsettling for the rhetoric of the Western humanitarian and point toward an ambivalence in the discourse? If if the slave is freed and, therefore, approximates an equal to his/her master, the slave's otherness is undercut. Because the rubric of discourses ripe with "civilizing" and "imperialist" projects relies on a racist logic used to justify the necessity of a white European or US guiding force, the freed, to some extent, destabilizes his/her status as other.

It is important to consider the stakes involved in such a textual and discursive contradiction. bell hooks is quick to remind us to look more closely into the abolitionists' outcry for reform. Suggesting that these writing subjects simply got caught in the rules of discourse fails to look more closely at the internalization of a naturalized racism. One is reminded of bell hook's assertion that there is an erroneous tendency "to equate abolitionism with a repudiation of racism" (hooks 124). hooks continues that white abolitionists "attacked slavery, not racism...While they strongly advocated an end to slavery, they never advocated a change in the racial hierarchy that allowed their caste status to be higher than that of black women or men" (125).

It is also important to point out that Tristan's insertion of anti-slavery commentary has certain rhetorical advantages for her call to end the universal plight of women. Her comparisons of slavery and unhappy yet indissoluble marriage serve her in her arguing for the equal rights of (white, bourgeois) women. After all, the issue of an exploitative marriage did not correspond to a slave's reality.

Tristan's analogies of the bitterly unhappy, exploited and "enslaved" wives in bad marriages are suspect. We can see this comparison of the Western "enslaved" wife to "the black slave" in several citations throughout her travelogue. For example, in her conversation with her cousin Carmen about the suffering of "women," Tristan professes to Carmen that "[e]n Europa como aquí, las mujeres están sometidas a los hombres y tienen que sufrir aún más su tiranía Pero en Europa se encuentran...mujeres a quienes Dios ha concedido suficientes fuerzas morales para sustraerse al yugo" (Tristan 211). Later, Tristan, in an implicit aside to the reader, makes known her new enlightened analysis of the situation though limited in scope: the horrors of the female slave left outof how universal woman's suffering is: "Las mujeres de acá, pensaba, son por el matrimonio tan desgraciadas como en Francia..." (211). Obviously, this analogy leaves out the specifics of the female slave's reality and fits what bell hooks considers to be a grossly inaccurate and self-serving comparison:

> Theoretically, the white woman's legal status under patriarchy may have been that of 'property,' but she was in no way subjected to the de-humanization and brutal oppression that was the lot of the slave. When white reformers made synonymous the impact of sexism on their lives, they were not revealing an awareness of or sensitivity to the slave's lot; they were simply appropriating the horror of the slave experience to enhance their own cause. (hooks 126)

In summing up the traits both male and female travel writers do share one notices that the European and North American texts under consideration here exhibit the same characteristics that Mary Louise Pratt has found in what she considers to be "capitalist vanguard" narratives. Pratt coins the term, "capitalist vanguard" to denote those narratives that tend to thematize and emphasize imperial expansionist designs (Pratt 148). Their manner of thematization fits what David Spurr calls "rhetoric of empire" in which racial and cultural differences in the peoples of a host society are represented in such a way by a foreign minority rhetorically "proving" the former's "inferiority" in need of the latter's "superior" expertise (Spurr 5). Poor administration, poor infrastructure, "uncouth" customs and racial diversity all mark Peru's "inferiority" according to the travel writers studied here.

Though male and female travel writers do share certan rhetorical characteristics, women writers do mark their difference from their male contemporaries in very "feminine" gendered ways. "Injecting gender" is Schriber's term which refers to how women travel writers emphasize their perspective as "feminine" and maximize their "femininity" in ways to authorize their travel texts and garner more agency for themselves as writing subjects. Whereas the discourse of male travel writers is proffered from an assumed transcendental and, therefore, assumed genderless position of the universal writing subject (what has been referred to as the Master Subject: white, Eurocentric, male), women writers were not afforded that luxury.

This is not to say that the Master Subject is not, in fact, gendered. As Trinh Minh-ha deconstructs it, we see that through the mask of the universal, transcendental "human" subject, which is actually the predominantly white Eurocentric male writing subject, the gendered quality of the Master Subject is obscured through the anonymity "humankind" affords "mankind": "What can such a word as 'human' mean when its collaboration with 'man' and 'men' throughout the history of mankind has become obvious? What can 'human experience' imply in a 'Men Only' context where we who are ourselves men study men?" (Minh-ha 66). Brought more specifically to the genre of travel writing, Shriber insists that men's writing becomes "normative" because they write as "a single universal male voice that reifies the canon," yet feminine gendered writing by women becomes a writing injected with a heavy dosage of "femaleness" (70).

The discourse of women travel writers exploits the outwardly injected, gender quality of their writing to their favor. Given that they come up against the essentialized and naturalized notion that woman is not the universal I of Knowledge and Tradition, they proffer their gender and its gendered knowledge, heretofore neglected, by the male writing subject. For example, Dahlgren sells the worth of her travelogue as offering a different perspective, uncharted by the male writing subject. Dahlgren, upon comparing her travel journal to that of her husband's, is clearly aware of what difference she is writing from: "These [journal entries of her husband] we do not propose to use in this narrative, but simply give our own impressions as they affect a *feminine mind*" (Dahlgren 58; my emphasis). She reaffirms this position with an even more modest tone, writing that she "hesitatingly ventures" to offer her travelogue as mere "scribbles." Nevertheless, ever-encouraged by the pluralization of the first person voice, she manages to overcome her hesitancy upon realizing that, "there is one niche, and one alone, left open for us, and that is a woman's gossiping sketches of social life, and her emotional views of things" (178).

Dahlgren and Tristan travelogues exhibit gender injections in two primary ways. First, they employ a doubly-layered use of the danger motif. Secondly, certain gendered injections occur when Dahlgren and Tristan attempt to soften their political commentaries. I refer to these attempts as textual curtsies.

Earlier in the chapter it was observed that both bourgeois men and women travelers participate in imperial discourse in some very similar ways without necessarily amplifying their gender. However, there are also points of divergence. One example of how the women writers inject gender is how the convention of the danger motif regarding the traveler's sea voyage to Peru, which allows the writing subject to inscribe himself or herself heroically, becomes maternalized in the case of the women. The purpose of the danger motif is to create interest through danger, through the arduousness encountered during one's adventures to an(other) world. As Schriber states it, "[t]ravel writers figure contemporary life in foreign lands as an obstacle...an element...that magnifies the courage and heroism of the traveler's persona" (Schriber 67). For Schriber, there exists a gendered difference in the nature of danger in a man's travel text versus a woman's travel text.

To set up how the convention works "traditionally" through the mask of a "universal human" subject and, therefore, an (un)markedly masculine way, the following quote from von Tschudi will be useful to analyze: "In those dangerous waters [of Cape Horn]...the waves rage more furiously than in any other part of the world...For twenty-two days we were driven about on the fearfully agitated sea, and were only saved from being buried in the deep by the excellent build and soundness of our ship" (von Tschudi 2). In one opening paragraph, the hero clearly exhibits a tenacity to survive great obstacles in order to bring to the reader the "truth" of (an)other land.

Both Blunt and Schriber notice differences in how the danger motif is represented in women's travel discourse. As Blunt puts it, "The conventions and constraints shaping travel writing are clearly gendered. For example, the role of heroic adventurer was available to a male narrator, but women were constrained by feminine codes of conduct" (Blunt 36).

Though I agree with Blunt and Schriber that a gendered difference does occur as in the case of Tristan and Dahlgren, their use of the danger motif cannot be completely bracketed off from the one evoked by their male contemporaries. Both Dahlgren and Tristan provide plenty of mention of the arduousness they encounter through their travels. Storms come up; ships rock violently; boat leakage occurs; obstacles are constant and are constantly overcome. The difference that I find in Tristan and Dahlgren as opposed to their male travel writing contemporaries is twofold, however. The first difference relates to the amount of textual space given to the environmental conditions of the passage: in terms of textual space allotted to the environmental obstacles, they provide them to a lesser degree. That is, by no means, to say they don't mention certain storms that came up and the consequences that arose as a result of stormy passage; both women do narrate bouts of rough weather during the ship-ride to Peru (Dahlgren 10; Tristan 31-33). The second difference that occurs is noteworthy, too, because these women writers supplement the danger motif with an additional element that forebodes not just the danger already withstood but also the danger lying ahead.

In Schriber's study of the texts she examined, danger in the female traveler's texts manifests itself in terms of the survival of a female's purity. My reading of the danger motif sees it as highly "feminized" as well; however, in the case of Dahlgren and Tristan, they do not so much play with the danger of maintaining their purity though Dahlgren does toy with it to a minimal degree. Instead, they maternalize the danger. In this way these two women writers incorporate another layer regarding the danger encountered during the passage over. They stress the danger specifically distressing to maternal travelers: what about their children's wellbeing?

For Tristan, her daughter comes up as a chance to express the anxiety involved in making the decision to leave her daughter in the hands of another trusted woman and family in France and to keep her from being in the custody of the villain, her husband. Tristan in fact relates to us the danger motif as a woman on the run and incognito from her husband in her preface before the passage to Peru even begins. Because the option of divorce had been abolished, the only way to free herself from an unfit marriage was to flee, disguising herself as a widow with children (Tristan 30-31). The villain is identified in the text early on: "Las persecuciones de Mr. Chazal me habían obligado, en distintas ocasiones, a huir de París" (31).

Referring to her husband as a literary villain is in no way intended to suggest the possibility that he wasn't also a literal villain for Tristan or to suggest that Tristan didn't have any real concerns regarding her children's welfare as well as her own from the violent behavior of her husband. Indeed, her husband André Chazal shot her in 1838 and was later imprisoned for his attempt on her life. However, I do wish to point out that his villainy serves her as a writing subject. It adds an additional layer of danger: the fear of her husband stalking her, or finding her daughter Tristan already having lost custody of her son.

In Tristan's text the danger motif is in some respects as much about the danger involved in procuring a passage out as it is about surviving the passage over seas to Peru and is filled with a sense of anxiety: "Dejar mi país que amaba con predilección; abandonar a mi hija que no tenía más apoyo que el mío...En fin, hacer todos esos sacrificios, afrontar todos esos peligros, porque estaba unida a un ser vil que me reclamaba como a su esclava" (36). There is the sense of foreboding over what kinds of repercussions she will face as well as those her children might have to confront as a result of her decision to go to Peru, leaving them behind while trying to wrest from her Uncle Pio her "rightful" yet undocumented claim to succession rights. In fact, her text is generated as much by the need to provide for her children as it is an escape from her husband; hence, her hopes of securing an ample inheritance. Once she realizes that the only way to procure her succession rights would be to fight her uncle in court, Tristan thinks of the possibility of unfavorable results for her children: "El interés de mis hijos subyugaba mi carácter...Tenía pocas probabilidades de triunfar...y con el proceso perdería también la protección que podría conceder a mis hijos" (32).

Due to the fact that Tristan's preface to her travelogue expresses the concerns and dangers she faced as a mother, the reader is immediately informed: Tristan presents herself to the reader as a mother first and a traveler second. Dahlgren's motherly evocations, in fact, appear even before she maternalizes the danger motif because she relates environmental obstacles through a figurative language derived from the care of children then considered "feminine" task. Early in her travelogue, Dahlgren uses metaphors that evoke motherhood, a principal form of gender injection according to Schriber. For example, when describing her passage over raging seas, Dahlgren uses a highly figurative language that evokes images of mothers and babes, from the way the sailors manage themselves, to the rocking of the vessel, to the exasperated passengers:

> ...[L]ittle do the gallant crew...take heed of all this sickening motion! Each man walks jauntily on his 'sea-legs,' with as easy a roll as if he were once again rocked in his mother's cradle! Walk, did I say? The cradle sings no lullaby, for the men scamper about the rigging as the vessel rolls even to the water's edge, and we grow faint as we think of it. (Dahlgren 19)

As regards the danger motif specifically in Dahlgren's text, her children, still very young must endure the trials of the passage over with her, and she must fight like a good mother to make certain they survive the trip. For example, once the steamer she's aboard leaves Panama, a fellow passenger warns Dahlgren that their boat will be detained at an area known to be a site ravaged with yellow fever. Her reaction is dramatic in its worry to safeguard her children: "We seek relief in tears, and weep bitterly. Already our infant children are gasping for breath in this heated air, and how prolong their precious lives in this sultry oven, under the molten, fiery sky?" (11). This fear for her children from yellow fever continues for pages approximately two thirds of the chapter with high drama: "our babies lie in an almost comatose state" (12); "our babes breathe more and more heavily" (13); "both infants were hopelessly ill" (14); "upon the thread of...flitting moments hangs the suspended life of our boy" (17). In fact, it isn't until Dahlgren and her children are able to find a more fitting American steamtug to continue their journey that her babies suddenly return to their vivacious selves:

> With a sense of untold relief, and fervent gratitude to God, bearing in our arms our almost dying child, we are placed in the captain's gig...By four o'clock the anchor is up...From this instant our children revive from their prolonged and dangerous stupor, and quickly regain their accustomed vivacity. (18)

Dahlgren triumphs as mother and protectress of her children, safeguarding them from yellow fever during the sea passage, so much so, that her children scarcely appear later in the text until, as if anxious to soften her political comments, she again introduces motherhood as purveyor of U.S. culture as we shall see later.

When one considers how the danger motif functions in the travelogues of these women writers, one notices how it becomes doubly loaded; it shares the "masculine" quality of surviving the seas and all the detriment that implies. Additionally, however, the impending doom is ever-amplified by the mother's concern for the welfare of her children.

Gender also comes into play in another discursive difference that concerns certain textual moments of anxiety over authority, especially when offering political commentary. Dahlgren and Tristan have different ways of overcoming those moments of anxiety.

Dahlgren's polite curtsy into the discussion of politics involves maximizing what agency republican motherhood of the era affords her. In fact, the image of motherhood filters through several chapters of Dahlgren's text as if to prepare the reader for her more "audacious" pleas for granting women increased official participation in a nation's politics. As noted earlier Motherhood serves Dahlgren in a number of ways: besides thickening the danger motif, it also softens what could be seen as an audacious insertion of political commentary in her text.

Several scholars have pointed out how nineteenth-century patriarchal discourses repeated the ideal of motherhood as an essentialized quality that limited women's identity and activity; however, due to liberal discourse's tenant of democratic representation for its citizenry, it was also necessary to assure (the bourgeois and elite) women that they fulfilled an important national role. Therefore, "motherhood" becomes an ambivalent construct: essentialized sign of woman impregnated with a political agenda. Dahlgren, then appropriates that sign to allow her increased agency, highly suggestible in its implication for garnering more outward political activity for U.S. women as ambassadors, informal as they might be. According to critics like Francine Masiello, Linda Kerber and Eva Cherniavsky, the discourse of Republican motherhood represented women as mothers with the task of inculcating nationalized moral values in their children, the future citizens of the nation.[3] Women were civil servants and educators to their children, limited to their own family unit.

Republican motherhood, then, was already a discourse fertile with politicized design in which women writers like Dahlgren were afforded the opportunity to plant and cultivate their own more liberating intentions, procuring what Mariam Johnson considers to be a form of maternal agency. According to Johnson, unlike the role of wife which undercut a woman's power, "motherhood, abstracted from marriage" is "associated with independent power and agency" (Johnson 153). Wherever there is a moment of ambivalence in discourse there is a space for resistance.

For Dahlgren, mothers are invested not only with national but moral authority: "Motherhood is the one most glorious crown of woman, through which she becomes invested with a dignity and an importance not only as a citizen, but also before High Heaven for whom she rears immortals!" (Dahlgren 196). Having authorized herself as a mother in a concrete sense through her use of the danger motif, she expands the national utility of mothers everywhere, extending it to the bounds of an admittedly informal but, nevertheless, political realm. Dahlgren manages this through an adept textual curtsy, using the guise of motherhood to soften what could be easily construed as an inappropriate and even audacious suggestion. Dahlgren touts motherhood as a tool more specifically for international relations. She does this by arguing that the language of motherhood is as diplomatic as it is universal: "As no other language is understood by Madame [wife of President Prado] than the stately Castilian, the conversation at first is somewhat embarrassed, until the motherly thought rises uppermost in our heart to ask to see the baby" (31).

Dahlgren later makes the connection that it is the interest of mothers that allows the meeting to go so smoothly, working more effectively as if deals could be better managed by "diplomatic lace" than by mere "red tape"—"lace" clearly being a gender-injected term. Dahlgren soon after appeals to a readership of mothers to consider the situation similarly should such an occasion arise: "We appeal to every mother who reads this, for we know perfectly well that their verdict will sustain our very informal management of foreign relations on this occasion" (32). First, dressed in a quaintly anecdotal context, this example is both an early and rather innocuous example of Dahlgren expanding the range of utility that a republican mother can offer to her country. It, nevertheless, reminds the reader that this text is written by a female writing subject.

Interestingly, Dahlgren becomes both more emphatic about how advantageous a woman's increased participation in foreign relations could be for her nation and boldly critical of what policies restrict her from doing so at the end of the travelogue. Whereas we first see Dahlgren's manipulation of motherhood to include a political flavor (informal as it is) embedded in a charming anecdote; at the end of the text, Dahlgren is more direct and assertive. For instance, disgruntled by the U.S.'s naval policy, which discourages the naval officer's families from joining them, Dahlgren disapproves of the navy's failure to provide housing for the officers' families. Often families remained separated from their naval husbands and fathers. Dahlgren first connects this lament to a more "acceptable" concern for the maintenance of her own family, but then expands it to argue again for women's role as female ambassadors paving the way for acceptance of the U.S.'s military, economic and cultural presence by reminding the reader that the people of a host country are frequently less suspicious of the foreign women:

> Our navy regulations discourage...any attempt of the families of officers to remain near the cruising ground of those near and dear to them...To our apprehension all this is a mistake. The American women are the best Christianizers, civilizers, and society diplomatizers the nation can employ. This is one of the functions our women may properly fill with benefit to the country. (98)

Dahlgren then offers a hypothetical example to demonstrate fully the advantage of offering government housing for the navy: "When an admiral or captain reaches port and has a house on shore...the people of that port welcome their return. They no longer think, 'This is a man-of-war come to spy out the land,' but they receive them as messengers of peace" (99).

Dahlgren's maternal tone and critique comes close to a tone of motherly states(wo)man abroad, for her criticism of her own nation's international policies extends to issues beyond the realm of granting women more participation as patriotic mothers. As mentioned previously, Dahlgren willingly chastises her government's lack of skills in negotiating better commerce practices with Peru (34; 103). She also admonishes the U.S.'s supply of men and weapons to countries not sufficiently evangelized and therefore still barbarian: "Let us first evangelize these people, before we rely so far on their good faith as to place murderous weapons within their control" (198). She even criticizes her government's choice of representatives sent to Peru, noting their incompetence: "The South Americans are generally able as diplomatists. We do not understand this particular bent of the genius of the people in the United States, and we are apt to send them mere politicians of a very mediocre calibre...Let us, then, be represented near these countries by men of keen perceptions..." (72).

The quote cited above is fast proceeded by what I consider a textual curtsy back into the parameters "acceptable" for a woman's textual place: she re-enters the salons of social life and comments on common phrases uttered by the Peruvian men and women with whom she visits. After condemning the U.S. politicians in Peru as mediocre, she quickly adds, "But to cease our philosophical reflections and re-enter the social limits, we propose to ourselves. We have had some considerable access to the inner circle of domestic life" (72-73). This appears to be a site of anxiety, the need to reinscribe onself into a more "gender appropriate" sphere from which to offer authority.

In addition to constantly associating the image of woman with that of patriotic mother, Dahlgren includes another female image in her text whose appearance seems to offer relief from any anxiety elicited from the fear involved in going too far to argue for a more politicized form of republican motherhood: the caricaturized vision of the women's liberationist.

Before looking at specific textual examples, it is important to understand a particular brand of subject anxiety two-fold in the case of the female subject. As Sandra Gilbert and Susan Gubar have pointed in their corrective to Harold Bloom's theory, not only does the female writing subject share in the "anxiety of influence" that her male counterpart experiences, that anxiety involved in trying to achieve not only the level of subject authority of their precursors but also of trying to exceed it; but additionally, she experiences another facet of anxiety, the "anxiety of authorship" in which the female subject experiences a multitude of insecurities, among them "her fear of the antagonism of male readers, her culturally conditioned timidity about self-dramatization, her dread of the patriarchal authority of art, her anxiety about the impropriety of female invention" (Gilbert and Gubar 50). All of these insecurities mark the female subject's text in a gendered way, "differentiat[ing] her efforts at self-creation from those of her male counterpart" (50).

How do moments of this "anxiety of authorship" come up in the texts of Dahlgren and Tristan? Such moments arise whenever the subjects feel the possible weight of being judged as women exhibiting gender impropriety, especially when inserting political commentary in their texts.

As if to assuage moments of textual anxiety Dahlgren incorporates intermittently the image of the "indignant, silly, and inappropriate" manners and pleas of the women's rightist. Each time she crops up, Dahlgren's tone is one of belittlement. As if in a moment of anxiety, advocating too much agency for women, Dahlgren brings in disparaging metaphors or quips about what Dahlgren refers to as "the women's-libber." For example, the dangerous turbulence involved in sea travel is likened to the temperament of an "indignant woman's-righter, who is too everlastingly demonstrative to adjust herself to a peaceful order of things" (19). Later, in the text, the image of the woman suffragist appears, approving of a manner of dress and activity considered highly "unladylike" by Dahlgren herself. Having already pointed out Dahlgren's racism, the comparison of the Chola to the woman-liberationist in the following quote strikes a tone of disapproval for both types of women: "And now comes the Chola wearing immense hoops. She too sits astride [her horse], in a free and easy way that would delight our woman's righter at home" (49). Similarly, in a chapter concerning Dahlgren's jaunt to Chile, upon representing the lifestyle of the Araucanians (later referred to as "savages"), the writing subject likens the practice of polygamy with other oppressive practices against women that a feminist platform (a "barbarous platform" in the words of Dahlgren) simply cannot resolve. According to Dahlgren, only Christianity can insure the rights of women within proper and "ladylike" parameters, of course:

> Polygamy, however, continues to prevail among these Indians, and their women must therefore be in a depressed and degraded state..., but this is invariably the status of woman unless protected by the Christian law, which alone grants all those privileges ever denied to her when she is placed to struggle for herself, upon the barbarous platform of 'equal rights.' Such a position for woman always results in the oppression of might; since she has a physical inferiority as to strength. (Dahlgren 116)

The image of patriotic mother (quietly resistant and negotiating for increased rights) and the women's liberationist (outwardly and undauntingly demanding equal rights) appear as two conflicting representations. Nevertheless, they seek something in common: increased mobility and political participation. Ironically, the vision of the suffragette comes to Dahlgren's discursive aid: she is there to assure any potentially disturbed reader that Dahlgren is not threateningly bent on equal rights, but rather inviting her nation to maximize her utility and service to her country through increased political participation.

Whereas Dahlgren brings in the indignant "women's libber" to her aid, Tristan brings in the "truth value" and proof of consent through her use of dialogue whenever the anxiety of female impropriety arises. Though Tristan seems undauntedly confrontational in her insistence that (bourgeois) women be considered as equals, she, nevertheless, softens her blatant protest through narrativized dialogue.

Upon a first preliminary reading of Tristan's text, it is easy to conclude too hastily that Tristan is fearless in her demands for women's rights. Her tongue will not be tamed. She condemns all manner of injustices brought up against the universalized faction known to her as WOMEN. Her social commentary is blatant: "En Europa como aquí, las mujeres están sometidas a los hombres y tienen que sufrir aún más su tiranía. Pero en Europa se encuentran...mujeres a quienes Dios ha concedido suficientes fuerzas morales para sustraerse al yugo" (Tristan 211).

However, upon further examination of her text, the reader notices how her social criticism or political commentary on the national affairs of Peru occurs embedded in quotations, in dialogues prompted by other protagonists. This practice of embedding her polical commentary within a narrativized dialogue maybe serves Tristan as writing-subject to soothe her anxiety of authority through the apparent consensus conveyed through dialogue in which other members participating in the conversation agree with her. The most obvious of these examples occurs in a chapter, subtitled. This occurs most obviously in two important chapters, one in which she flings a diatribe against indissolubility of marriage and how it serves to enslave women ("Don Pío de Tristán y su familia"); the other in which Tristan participates wholly with assumed authority in a discussion about the political unrest in Peru ("La República y los tres presidentes").

In "Don Pío..." the reader overhears a conversation Tristan has with her cousin, Carmen another unhappily wed woman. It is at this point in the text where Tristan asserts most clearly the "universal" plight of (bourgeois) women everywhere who are stuck in a loveless marriage that binds them into an economic form of slavery. In fact, it is Tristan's cousin who opens up the conversation. After surviving an earthquake together, Carmen jeers, "loathsome country," provoking curiosity in Tristan to ask Carmen why she stays. Thereafter, Tristan admits freely to the reader, " Las mujeres de acá, pensaba, son por el matrimonio tan desgraciadas como en Francia..." (211).

When Tristan turns her attention to politics in Peru, especially in chapter ten, dialogue appears throughout. Again as noted in the section above with

Carmen, another protagonist serves as actant to Tristan's entry into political discussions. Both her uncle Pio, a politician himself, and her cousin, Althaus, a mercenary to the Peruvian military, come to Tristan for advice once conflicting reports and legitimacy of a new Peruvian president (President Orbegoso) is announced, adding to the conflicting two presidents already fighting for power and legitimacy (President Gamarra and President Bermúdez). Both male relatives consult Flora as to which of the presidents (President Bermúdez or President Orbegoso) they should proclaim their loyalty to.

What a flattering and authorizing situation for Tristan! From the lips of don Pio's mouth, we hear how highly he esteems Tristan's political acumen: "Mi querida Florita. Aconséjeme. Usted tiene apreciaciones tan justas en todo y es realmente la única persona aquí con la cual puedo hablar de cosas tan graves" (41). Soon afterwards, Althaus comes to her for advice: should he sign on as military officer under the newly declared president (Orbegoso) or stay with the army under President Bermúdez' command: "'Florita, no sé que hacer. ¿Por cuál de estos tres bribones de presidentes debo tomar partido'" (42). Not only do her male relatives confide in her for advice, but they proceed according to her views and come back afterwards satisfied with the outcome and grateful. Tristan's uncle comes back to her, "content," her proof in dialogue: "Ah! Florita, ¡Qué bien he hecho en proceder según sus consejos!" (45).

Though this chapter begins with a dialogue that invites Flora into the discussion of Peru's political chaos of the time, after the dialogue terminates, Tristan is able to expound further as a narrator. She goes on to pinpoint Peru's problems as a nation and profess where and why it fails. However, Tristan ends her commentary with a peculiarly anxious phrase to assure the reader that she is forced into such commentary. After several pages of Tristan's rhetorical ruminations, she reminds the reader that such commentary was solicited by those around her as if an anxious need arose to justify her lengthy political posturing. It was imperative that she discuss politics because as she puts it, "En vano hubiera tratado de huir de las conversaciones sobre política. En casa de mi tío la política era el tema de todas las charlas" (47).

This inclusion of dialogue and its "proof" that Tristan was invited into the discussion of politics is a curtsy through quoted speech, a well-mannered, guarded entry into what was considered to be a male topic of discussion: national politics. No matter her revolutionary message, she is a writing subject "inferiorized" by the patriarchal climate that surrounds her. Therefore, there is still cause for textual moments of anxiety, or more specifically in Gilbert and Gubar's terms, moments of "anxiety of authorship" occluding the female writing subject from complete ease of expression (Gilbert and Gubar 50).

Both Tristan and Dahlgren, like other women travelers of their generation, "echoed the ethnocentrism of their society while questioning aspects of imperial policy and opening popular minds to the nonwestern world" (Strobel 39). However, upon considering the construction of female social reformer in these women's travelogues, one sees clearly that Dahlgren and Tristan go their separate ways in their efforts to secure more rights for the bourgeois woman: Tristan is adamant and openly confrontational in arguing for women's rights; whereas Dahlgren would probably find in Tristan the consummate "women's libber" she frequently evokes and pokes fun of in her text. Though both employ many of the same racist and imperialist discourses of othering techniques and do, indeed, inject their female gender into their narratives, they are, nevertheless, clear in their differences. One easily heeds Blunts warning regarding the study of women travel writers during this period: "...in the context of nineteenth-century patriarchal discourses, each woman traveler was very much an individual" (35).

In this chapter we have looked at how more general travel discourse conventions are localized to the site of Peru, and how men and women travel writers from imperial centers manipulate those conventions to authorize themselves as travel-writing subjects. In chapter three, we will look at how the Peruvian travel writers refashion many of the conventions discussed her to implicitly if not explicitly talk back to various centers simultaneously.

Notes

1. Tristan's work was originally published in French as *Meemoires et pérégrinations d'une paria* in 1838.

2. In her study of the male traveler subjects categorized as part of the capitalist vanguard, Pratt includes a chart of various races found in W. B. Stevenson's *Narrative of Twenty Years Residence in South America* (1825) exemplifying how imperialist discourse is laden with a "normalizing, homogenizing rhetoric of inequality" (Pratt 153).

3. See Cherniavsky (vii-xiii); Kerber (265-88); and Masiello (34-36).

• CHAPTER FOUR •

Talking Back to Center(s)

Imperialist travel writers employed certain representational techniques of "othering" to authorize themselves as subjects, simultaneously authorizing their home countries as "superior" to the Peruvian culture. Those techniques allowed them to set up a dichotomy in which their (North American or European) countries of origin inhabited the "civilized, modern, progressive" side of the division; whereas Peruvian society remained in a state of "premodernity." Rhetorically "proving" Peru's "need" for North American or European intervention, those techniques centered around negative signifiers: Peru's poor infrastructure, poor administration, "uncouth" customs and diverse racial make-up of the population, represented as a sign of degradation.

But what about the Peruvian travel writers? In their push to authorize themselves as subjects, did they engage in similar tropes that would pinpoint national "others"? How did their representations of Peruvian culture and reality differ from those we examined in the previous chapter? What kind of political criticism did they give forth? And to whom did they direct it? Were their criticisms multidirectional? Like the women writers looked at previously, did they maximize their travelogues not just to talk back to imperial centers but to their own nation's capitol, Lima, as well? These are questions this chapter seeks to explore according to two parts.

The first part of the chapter examines those tropes which the Peruvian writers, Manuel Anastacio Fuentes, Juan Bustamante and José Manuel Valdéz y Palacios, engage in like their North American and European contemporaries. This examination, however, will entail a look at how those tropes become socially accented according to a discursive push to present Peru as a nation in charge of its own destiny, autonomous and worthy of being recognized by other world leaders. Heteroglosia haunts the tropes in that embedded in them lies antagonism. The utterance of regional Peruvian travelers "contains within it the trace of other utterances" past and future of the foreign travelers to whom they find themselves responding.[1]

Therefore, signifiers will be examined according to two desires. The first concerns the issue of how the writing subjects try to present Peru as autonomous and nationally distinct while still comparable to other progressive nations and, therefore, worthy of participating in the world economy, a message directed to talk back to North American and European representations of Peru. The second issue for these subjects involves the added desire to present themselves as subjects representative of the Creole or Mestizo class most "civilized" and, therefore, "best prepared" to guide the nation. Whereas Pratt noticed a similar appropriation of tropes (what she considers to be a form of Creole refashioning) in the poetry of Latin American writers, this chapter will note a similar function in the following texts: Valdéz y Palacios' Viaje de Cuzco a Belén (1846); Fuentes' Lima: Apuntes históricos, descriptivos, estadísticos y de costumbres (1867); and Bustamante's Viaje al Antiguo Mundo (1849).[2]

The second part of this chapter will examine an additional form of talking back which is on a regional level. Because the three works highlighted in this section were written during Peru's post-independence period, the nation was involved in a process of of trying to build a national hegemony that gravitated toward the nation's Creole sector in the capital, Lima. However, Andean Creoles and Mestizos were also engaged in trying to achieve authority, but found the region that they represented ignored and neglected by the capital. This exposes another conflict of interests between the limeño and serrano elites. Fuentes' text is indicative of the former, while the texts of Bustamante and Valdéz y Palacios correspond to the latter. Therefore, this chapter will include a discussion of the two levels of talking back that take place in the serrano texts, since Bustamante and Valdéz y Palacios not only talk back to European and North American imperialists, but also to limeño nationalists who have failed to incorporate the serrano people into its very young and precarious national imaginings.

Whereas the Serrano texts are clearly travel narratives, the case of Fuentes' work is different due to its proclivity toward cuadros de costumbres and its classificatory sketches. On the surface Fuentes' text may appear to be in a genre apart from travel literature. However, costumbrismo as a whole, especially taken into consideration with travelogues of the period, is not a genre so easily split off. A comparison of travel narratives and costumbrista texts of the period is useful here.

Comparatively both travel and costumbrista narratives are largely hybrid genres Looking first at travel writing, upon his consideration of travel narratives in Latin America, Jason Wilson defines it as: "A genre approach reveals the travel book to be an eclectic and refreshing hybrid of memoir, essay and autobiography in the realist mode, dealing with a verifiable place, and with an identifiable narrator" (Wilson 803). Considering Enrique Pupo-Walker's definition of Latin American costumbrista texts, one finds how strikingly similar the two are in terms of their hybrid nature. Pupo-Walker emphasizes the multiple blending of different discourses within a costumbrista work, making it a genre replete with a "stubborn resistance to definitions":

The costumbristas narrative...blends autobiographical information with satirical remarks, while incorporating quotations from journalistic sources, bits of poetry and traces of popular culture...Moreover, the costumbrista narrative is all too often an act of narrative mediation in which other discourses—historical, political or scientific—are mixed and dissolved into the trappings of a particular story. (492-499)

This observation is applicable to Peru as well. The curious departure is the absence that costumbrista writing was a journalistic writing that often required traveling to particular regions for producing cuadros about particular tipos of people within the homeland or country.

There is an inherent connection between travel literature and some costumbrista texts during the nineteenth century since costumbristas had in their intent to categorize all the tipos within their homeland's boundaries whether inhabiting urban centers or rural landscapes.[3] In his study of Cuban costumbrista writers Bueno affirms that "[t]odas las zonas del país, los más diversos segmentos de la sociedad colonial, las profesiones y los oficios, las costumbres urbanas y rurales, los personajes más curiosos, acumulan su anacrónica estampa en estos cuadros y bocetos" (Bueno xiv).

On the road for their profession to capture rural life and costumes, many costumbrista writers include albeit briefly within their narratives their travel to a particular region within colonial or national boundaries. Some Cuban cases demonstrate this point. In J.V. Betancourt's "Los curros del manglar" the subject briefly mentions "rebaladizo terreno" through which he must "hacer [su] excursiones" in order to produce his text (Betancourt 261). Similarly José Quintín Suzarte's "Los guajiros" involves a narrator who assures the reader he/she does not have to "hacer tan largo y penoso viaje" because the author has obliged himself to take that task on for the reader's benefit (Suzarte 415). Even if we follow the itenary of the titles of the Peruvian costumbrista, Felipe Pardo y Aliaga, we see the necessity of travel for some costumbrista topics: "Una huérfana en Chorrillos"; "El Carnaval de Lima"; "Un viaje"; and "El paseo a Amancaes" (Cornejo Polar 64-65). Paul Verdevoye mentions how Sarmiento's travels through South America helped him pinpoint his reformist criticisms of poor infrastructure between Santiago and Valparaíso in his costumbrista articles (Verdevoye 69).

Another strain of similarity in the discourses often incorporated within both genres in the inclusion of scientific taxonomic gesturing. Just as the foreign travelers such as von Tschudi, Carleton and Dalhgren point out the different races and types of Peruvian peoples to be found, so too did the costumbristas point out national tipos within the confines of their country or homeland. A characteristic of nineteenth-century travel writing influences by eighteenth and nineteenth-century scientific discourses which travel theorists such as Spurr and Pratt have examined in their research.[4] Likewise, Pupo-Walker's investigations of costumbrista texts highlight the same penchant for taxonomic writing (Pupo-Walker 496; 499-503).

Latin Americanists such as Jean Franco, Antonio Cornejo Polar and John Brushwood point out that Latin American costumbrismo like its Spanish counterpart often has a reformist quality to it to point out flaws in the nation in favor of correction, administrative or cultural.[5] Imperialist travelers to Peru also rhetorically manipulated Peru's need for reform to justify imperial intervention.

In summary both genres of travel and costumbrista narratives of the period shares many points of common interest: both are hybrid genres in which essay, autobiography and memoir are interwoven with anecdotal stories; both share a taxonomic penchant to point out the customs and tipos found throughout the travels recounted; both involve narration in a realist mode; both center around verifiable locations; both involve traveling through various regions, underscored in the travel narrative while implicit in some costumbrista pieces and explicit in others.[6] The main difference between them is that in travel narratives the process of traveling is foregrounded wheras in costumbrista texts the anecdotal information picked up while in different regions is underscored rather than the journey itself.

Perhaps since as Wilson puts it "what constitutes travel literature is still being defined" the costumbrista connection is lost (803). This disregard of regional travel could be attributed possibly to Western tradition's esteem of the heroic traveler who adventures off to an/other land. Whereas costumbrista writing entails regional travel, it does not entail travel of mythic proportions, travel capitalized, Travel. It lacks the heroic traveler of Joseph Campbell's monomythic adventure story which requires "a passage beyond the known into the unknown" (Campbell 82).[7] Such a myopic focus on the traveler who ventures to a distant land undercuts the possibility of finding travel writing traditions elsewhere. In fact examining regional travel literature is an important resource for several reasons.

First, it allows for the rethinking of travel writing as a genre and for the consideration of a different type of traveling hero: the republican adventurer exposing national regions left out of nation-building projects in nineteenth-century Latin America. Just as Anderson found that Creole functionaries began building a sense of horizontal comradeship during the late colonial period—serving as precursor connections in pre-independence Latin America -, early republican regional travel writers were at work in national imaginings and connecting regions—early voices in the attempts to solidify a nascent country (Anderson 57). Secondly, an equally important allure of studying regional travelogues is its resource in finding not only national voices but serving as evidence in refuting such claims that "[t]here is not a strong tradition of Latin American empirical observation or of Latin American travel writing, and even less on traveling within the Latin American continent" (Wilson 803).

In view of these points of shared discourses and narrative intentions, the inclusion of Fuentes' text is fitting and offers a distinctly Lima-centered perspective of what in his view constitutes those national Peruvians best equipped to run the young nation, leaving Andean peoples in the role of tipos, national others, who have immigrated to Lima for whatever reason. Additionally, from the commencement of his work, Fuentes keeps the foreign traveler in mind and offers his work as authoritative and able to correct the misrepresentations of Peruvian culture published by foreign travelers.

Whether or not the costumbrista narrators directly mention their own travels, often travelers are either a presence in their texts or directly confronted for their slighting representations of Latin American lands. Often costumbrista writers talk back to foreign travel writers who other the lands traveled to. This, too, connects the Serrano travelogues with Fuentes' work for the purposes of this chapter.

Upon first examination of the tropes used by Peruvian writers, one might assume that they reiterate the very conventions that we saw in imperialist travel writing. To some extent this is true; however, the goal is clearly different and socially accented from the locus of Peruvian nationalists seeking to present their nation and national culture as autonomous and distinct, while simultaneously comparable to other "civilized and progressive" nations. The bind how to present Peruvian culture as equally worthy as those cultures found in imperialist nations while still maintaining Peruvian distinction on an autonomously national level—lies at the heart of the ambivalence in these Peruvian travelogues.

Peruvian writers were aware of how the imperialist imagination had misrepresented Peruvian culture as "degraded" and in "desperate need" of imperialist intervention at all levels. Fuentes explicitly addresses how European travelers, especially contribute to the problems of misrepresenting Peru through a selectivity of anecdotal experiences and its narrow focus attuned only to picking up negative traits. In his first paragraphs of his prologue to Lima, Fuentes admits that misrepresentation of host countries is a common problem, regardless of the traveler and his/her destination. He lists several hypothetical examples (a Frenchman who travels to Spain; an Englishman who travels to Paris; and a German traveling to London) which reflect a mounting corpus of travel writing during the period. Each of these hypothetical travelers' gaze is skewed and, therefore, misinterprets customs due to not understanding cultural meanings and contexts. In the very first sentence of his prologue, he provides an example: "Un viagero francés á Madrid en el momento en que dos mozos crúos sostenian una lucha, cuchillo en mano; el viagero sacó, en el acto, su libro de memorias y escribió: 'A las doce del dia todos los españoles se dan de navajasos'" (iii; author's emphasis).

Though never dropping names, Fuentes moves to a localized example regarding French traveler's written perceptions of Peruvian culture:

> Los viageros, de diversas nacionalidades, que, en estos últimos años, han escrito algo sobre el Perú, parece que hubieran propuesto describir lo que debió ser años ántes de la conquista. Ahora mismo se publica en Paris una obra sobre viages que, si se juzga de la verdad de las noticias referentes á varios pueblos del mundo, por la de las que tocan al Perú, puede decirse que sus autores pretenden escribir una novela cuyos personages tengan todos el tipo grosero del salvage. (vi)[8]

Fuentes' quote reaffirms what poststructuralist and postcolonialist theorists have often pointed to: the immense power that haunts discourse and representation. It also alludes to the fact that, in order to represent Peru as backward and savage, imperialist travelers fixed their gaze inproportionally and racistly on the lower classes and the ethnic groups other than the elite and Creole Peruvians. Fuentes was not offended necessarily by the racism; he was offended by the immense focus on indigenous and African-Peruvians, which, according to the Creole nationalist, should not be in charge of representing the majority of Peruvians.

Though Fuentes never exposes the names of travelers outright, Dahlgren's travelogue, indeed, offers us a very specific example:

> Just previous to our arrival in Lima, a very clever bagatelle, Carlton we believe, had been published in New York, called 'Our Artist in Peru,' filled with humorous but absurdly exaggerated sketches of life in Lima...This trifle had made its way to the polite salons of Lima, and we perceive that society is very indignant over it. They complain to us, 'It is not true.' We answer, 'No, it is a caricature.' They answer again, with an offended shrug, 'Como no.' (73-74)

This example also alludes to how circles of literate Peruvians were aware, offended, and concerned at how their nation and people were being presented by foreign travelers. In fact, the Peruvian intellectual/writer was painfully aware of his/her problematic identity. Benedict Anderson addresses the problematic identity of the Creole in South America, terming it "the fatality of transAtlantic birth:

> Even if [the creole] was born within one week of his father's migration, the accident of birth in the Americas consigned him to subordination—even though in terms of language, religion, ancestry, or manners he was largely indistinguishable from the Spain-born Spaniard. There was nothing to be done about it; he was irremediably a creole...born in the Americas, he could not be a true Spaniard.... (Anderson 58)[9]

One might have been born of European parents, but he/she was tainted by his/her place of birth, a prodigy of the "New" World, an/other world whose "newness" automatically put it at a disadvantage on the linear timeline gauging Progress. Though Anderson—in the above quote—is focussing on the relationships of status inside the system of Spanish administration in its colonies just prior to the independence movements, European and U.S. American imperialists continued to view Creoles as contaminated by their place of birth. This is partly due to the enormous popularity of theories of climate—produced in the 1700s by George Louis Leclerc Buffon and Cornelius de Pauw—that posited that a man or woman born to the "New World" was "inevitably" and "naturally" made inferior by the climate that surrounded and contaminated him/her (Gerbi 53-54). Though climate theories which naturalized the supposed inferiority of Americans came out in the 1700s, their impact continued throughout the 1800s. In fact, one writer, William Robertson, who distilled and combined both Buffon and de Pauw's theories in his History of America (1777) was lauded by von Humboldt. Gerbi notes that von Humboldt considered Robertson's work "a classic and in 1827 gave his encouragement to a new edition of it in French" (158-159).

The stigma of being born in a New World country, especially a Latin American one is at the core of the crisis one finds in the Creole locus of enunciation. It is a crisis of identity that manifests itself within the goal of representing "we the Peruvians" in contrast to the Europeans yet still showing the nation of Peru as one exemplifying the goal of the nation: "progress," a goal assumed as a "universal" (yet "inherently" Western/European) sign.

The problem for the Peruvian Creole desiring to present Peru as both an autonomous and culturally distinct and worthy nation is how to represent Peru's distinct flavor without alienating it from Western Europe as "other" while at the same time maintaining its sense of cultural distinction.

As if Peru's status as an "indolent" and "backward" nation didn't make representing Peru as a nation worthy of participating in the world economy a difficult proposition, the task is exacerbated furthermore by a quandry inherent to any nationalist discourse. Partha Chatterjee writes that "Nationalist thought, in agreeing to become 'modern' accepts the claim to universality of this 'modern' framework of knowledge. Yet it also asserts the autonomous identity of a national culture" (Chatterjee 11).[10] A precarious discursive balance must be maintained for the Peruvian subject: he must stress the qualities of Peruvians that signify their membership in the construct of universal humanity on the one hand, while equally maintaining qualities distinctly Peruvian. For the national subject working within the ambivalence of nationalist discourse, he struggles to represent Peru as autonomous in national identity yet still compatible with the modern claim to universality.

This fragile balance helps to contextualize the Peruvian subject's constant alternation of comparing Peru to Europe and contrasting it to Europe in ways that refute imperialist representations of Peru. Examples of this comparison/contrast motif centers on Peru's geography, inhabitants and architecture. Bustamante plays with putting Inca centers on a par with other world cultural centers. One finds this most often when he describes Inca architecture. For instance while describing sites in the city of Cuzco, Bustamante gives laudatory descriptions of Sacsay-Guaman (an Inca Fortress) and the Templo del Sol (also known as the convent of Santo Domingo), putting such sites on a par with ancient Roman culture, authorizing himself through the quote of another Latin American traveler:

> Fundamento tuvo el viajero colombiano, el Sr. O'Leary, al hablar de esa ciudad [de Cuzco]...'Esta ciudad puede con razón llamarse la Roma de la América. La inmensa fortaleza en al lado del norte de la ciudad es un capitolio, y el templo del sol su coliseo. Manco Cápac fué su Rómulo; Viracocha su Augusto; Hauscar su Pompeyo, y Altahualpa su César.' (Bustamante 40)

Valdéz y Palacios constantly engages in this technique. Regarding Peru's Andean landscape, he first exalts the Andes as comparable to the Swiss Alps in terms of their majesty, but afterwards mentions that their fecundity is matched nowhere else in the world. At such point the comparison no longer serves him: "Imposible sería infundir con palabras una idea del contento y abudancia que hay en estas quebradas" (Valdéz y Palacios 26) Later Valdéz y Palacios compares Andean women to virginal women one finds in Byron's poetry and industrious workers harvesting crops that would rival a European work ethic; however, he still manages to set apart the Peruvian workers with their white jackets and straw hats: "Entre ellas están sentados los hombres, vestidos con sus chaquetas blancas y sus sombreros de paja y con unas maneras que un ciudadano de París no hubiera imaginado, ocupados todos en desmoronar el maíz con tal afán y prisa que se les podría tomar por los obreros de Oxford y Manchester" (30).

This technique of consistently comparing Peru to Europe and contrasting it to Europe in ways that attested to Peru's worthiness is one way the Peruvian subject implicitly talks back to imperialist centers. However, the Peruvian subjects studied in this chapter, also borrowed and refashioned some of the tropes we examined in chapter two in their efforts   the objective   clearly being different.

Earlier in chapter two, it became apparent that one trope of "othering" involved looking at customs and behaviors considered uncouth to the imperialist eye. Whereas the imperialists focussed on customs that would indicate a lack of modern civilization, Peruvian writers sometimes discussed the very same customs but constructing them as positive signifiers of national customs. Here I will consider one custom that von Tschudi, Dahlgren and Tristan had all used to point out an uncouth Peruvian population, the popular festivals. For the Peruvian writers, popular festivals are saturated with nationalism, not with signs of barbarism. Then I will bring in a discussion of the conventional discussion of the largely upper class women of Lima, las tapadas. Both of these discussions of customs lend clarity on how utterance is saturated with different agendas.

What imperialists represented as carnivalized behavior at festivals, Valdéz y Palacios represents in a positive light whether describing religious festivals or simply rural banquets that bring the community together. Valdéz y Palacios willingly admits that the table is set differently than in Europe and that the people are less reserved, but he applauds that difference because it marks a specifically Peruvian resource in its people: a natural sense of fraternity and affection: "Nada puede igualar al cariño y la fraternidad que reinan y los chistes y ocurrencias conceptuosas que animan estos banquetes rurales" (28). Anticipating that an European observer would disapprove, Valdéz y Palacios writes it as a flaw, a deficiency in the European that expresses itself as absence, the denial of a universal tendency of celebrating humanity:

> Quedaría espantada una lady aristocrática y se pondría muy serio un excéntrico gentleman viendo a las señoras de la clase más elevada no desdeñar ofrecer alguna cosa delicada a un amigo de distinción. Y, no obstante, no hay en esto nada que disminuya la pureza de su alma. Tan cierto es que la etiqueta y el exterior no forman el fundamento de la moral. (28;   author's emphasis)

What Valdéz y Palacios does is present caricatures of the aristocratic Europeans so aghast, serious and excentric, offsetting the words, lady and gentleman in bold type. Other textual instances also involve this spin on popular celebration carnivalized negatively in the imperialist texts for what is represented with a tone of universal humanity in Valdéz y Palacios.

Bakhtin noted the universal meaning attached to unofficial feasts: "universality lies in human life and work triumphing in the bounty of humankind's efforts to sustain itself through food: the triumphal banquet is always universal. It is the triumph of life over death" (Bakhtin, Rabelais and His World 229). This is not to suggest that some of the same carnivalizing signifiers don't appear in Valdéz y Palacio's text; they do: the couples dancing are engaged in a "frenesí o delirio," filled with "éxtasis," "fuego," and "locura" (34). The socially accented difference lies in the fact that this scene does not inspire repugnance in the observer (as it would in the imperialist texts) but rather an awe of beauty: "¡Qué escena de belleza tan particular ofrece esta reunión campestre a los ojos del observador!...¡Con qué expresión de placer no se fijarían los ojos de un epicúreo en aquella muestra de universal y sincero contento...!" (35). In fact, Valdéz y Palacio's comments about the festivals he observes in the sierra region of the nation indicate a haunting of imperialist representations written earlier about such festivals. Instead of agreeing with the notion that such activities are uncouth, Valdéz y Palacios places negativity on the side of the imperialist: it is the deficiency of celebratory humor and lack of tolerance in the European's severity and reserved nature that keeps him from valuing the warmth and fraternity of the human race.

Bakhtin explains that the celebration of the feast and the carnivalized nature that accompanies it belongs to a canon of the body that existed in the Middle Ages which corresponded to a celebration of universality that a more modernized version of the body leaves behind. In the modern canon of the body, connection to greater societal and cosmic whole is nullified: "In the modern image of the individual body, sexual life, eating, drinking, and defecation have radically changed their meaning: they have been transferred to the private and psychological level where their connotation becomes narrow and specific, torn away from the direct relation to the life of society and to the cosmic whole" (Bakhtin, Rabelais 229). This permits a two-fold consideration of what a portrayal of carnivalized activities could offer the travel writer: the feast and other carnivalized activities could be represented in such a way to stress universal humanity or as indicators of a nation frozen in a backwards time reminiscent of the Middle Ages. One is reminded here of how Tristan had to turn her head away ("apart[ó] los ojos con disgusto") from all the "crude" dancing that occurred during various religious festivals, equating it to behavior fitting for the "Dark Ages" (213-214).[11] Whereas the imperialists focus on the latter, the Peruvian subjects accentuate the former.

In order to not rely solely on the universal quality in the Peruvian people at the sake of diminishing their national uniqueness, Valdéz y Palacios is quick to stress two signifiers of Peruvian originality and culture, both offered from a

Serrano locus of enunciation: the yaraví and the Andean woman enchanted by the yaraví's melody and message. Valdéz y Palacios defines the yaraví as follows: "El yaraví es una canción en la que se expresan con un carácter original las quejas y los tormentos de amor" (36). The subject around which the yaraví centers provides the perfect discursive vehicle for Valdéz y Palacios to insert nationalized patrimony. Within the universal of Love, he is able to exalt both the Serrano woman and the yaraví.

In his explanation of the yaraví, the technique of comparison/contrast to European cultural models continues to play an important role. After first affirming that the yaraví addresses the universal, Love, Valdéz y Palacios goes on to describe it according to what European models it doesn't follow. It is neither like the complicated and passionate music of Italy; nor is it akin to the spiritualist hymns of German music. It has a tenderness and melancholy incomparable:

> Tienen [los versos y las notas] en tal modo una expresión de sentimiento y melancolía que no hay en el mundo una música y canciones que puedan ser comparadas…La alta y complicada música de las sociedades civilizadas de Europa, esa música de los grandes maestros de la Italia apasionada y de la Alemania espiritualista es sombría y es al mismo tiempo hija del genio y del arte…El yaraví es, por el contrario, una música de la naturaleza. (37)[12]

The writing subject is quick to point out that the natural quality of the yaraví is not to be considered savage, but rather sublime and pure: it constitutes a music, "no de la naturaleza salvaje, pero de la naturaleza en su pura armonía; es el primer suspiro del corazón, de un corazón que tuvo su origen en una melodía creada para el amor" (37).

After first relating a definition of the yaraví and describing its melody and message as well as the beauty of the women who listen to it, he offers the reader a scene that brings all elements together in the specifically Andean setting, subtitled, "Una noche de amor en los valles de la quebrada" (40). Before painting the scene, he asks with a tone of amazement: "¿Por qué no fue dado a Rafael contemplar una noche cara a cara este cuadro de tanta belleza para trasladarlo al lienzo con su pincel?" (40).

Valdéz y Palacios takes up the pincel himself, the task left to the Peruvian to represent his native region of the country. He stresses the originality of the music and the exotic beauty of the "muchacha americana" who listens to it, taking up the representation of it, since no European artist had thought to do so: "¡El Yaraví! ¡Melodía original e inimitable del nuevo mundo! ¡Y las ninfas originarias de los campos de América escuchandolo en una noche voluptuosa..!" (41).

According to Valdéz y Palacios, el yaraví is not just a distinctly Peruvian musical form, it is a distinct communicative form of expression which exceeds all other art forms when the message being conveyed involves love. European authors cannot compare to the kind of expressive quality that the yaraví produces:

> Ni Spencer, ni Catulo, ni Tíbulo, ni Guidi, ni Celio Magmo, pueden describir lo que son las sensaciones que producen en el alma las armonías del yaraví; ni pueden ellos llevar a la poesía esos transportes de delirio en que el alma se extasía. (38)

And what of this "muchacha americana" enraptured by the yaraví? She like the yaraví is incomparable to women found elsewhere. She, too, affirms a national originality. Regarding her charms, Valdéz y Palacios writes:

> Cuando un extranjero ha habitado entre aquellas americanas por algún tiempo y viene el destino después a arrancarlo de los jardines donde ellas forecen de esos valles protegidos por las montañas de los Andes, parece que ha huido de él para siempre la felicidad; y, caminando por las demás regiones del globo, cree que no encontrará iguales caricias como las que mereció de la mujer americana, ni armonías semejantes a las del quejumbroso yaraví. (39)

Though he generalizes the woman as "la americana," he specifies later in the text la mujer americana por excelencia: she is most like the cuzqueña or the urubambina, She is not to be confused with the "classic" woman of Western culture: "Allí están las cuzqueñas y urubambinas con sus púpilas revolteando en sus órbitas y sus miradas que no expresan, como en Esmirna o en Grecia una voluptuosa languidez, sino una pasión fogosa y expresiva" (52).

Interestingly, Valdéz y Palacios' "mujer americana" is not the exoticized woman found in imperialist texts, nor is she the representative Peruvian beauty according to Fuentes. When many authors comment on the Peruvian woman por excelencia as represented by the limeña (von Tschudi, Lastarria, Fuentes, Tristan, Dahlgren), Valdéz y Palacios chooses to celebrate the serrana. Rather the Peruvian woman that appears most frequently in the imperialist texts as well as in texts written from a locus of Peru's center, Lima, is the reknowned tapada which we will now examine.

Some Peruvian subjects use the tapada limeña- the Lima woman sporting the saya y mantoto emphasize nationalist originality and patrimony. Frequently, North American and European male writers represented the tapada in such a way as to denote Peruvian exoticism and neglect; whereas their female contemporaries represented her in a way which denoted freedom and equality for women. However, Fuentes manipulates the sign of the tapada to talk back to European and North American imperialists.

In order to better analyze how the Peruvian gaze appropriates the tapada's identity for nationalist purpose, we should first note how her inclusion into travel narratives worked conventionally in the narratives of North American and European travel writers. Scholars such as Pratt have noted that the upper class women from Lima, Peru dressed in their sayas y mantos generated a great deal of attention in the travel narratives of European and North American men and women alike during the 1800's. However, the representation of the tapada resulted from how each traveler's gaze was imbricated by certain agendas, corresponding to each traveler's personal or cultural allegiances. In this way, the sign of the limeña tapada exhibits the Bakhtinean notion of how utterance is socially accented. That is to say, the sign of the tapada is saturated with social context. It becomes a site "for the clash and criss-crossing of differently oriented social accents" (Bakhtin, *Marxism and the Philosophy of Language* 41). Therefore, regardless of each travel writer's place of origin, the tapada signifies different agendas: she signifies an strangely exoticized neglect for the male European and North American writers such as von Tschudi and Carleton; a site for arguing for increased women's rights for the female European and North American writers such as Tristan and Dahlgren; and a site for asserting a nationally autonomous culture for Fuentes.

The traveler's gaze often makes bodyscapes out of the peoples they represent (Spurr 25). As such, the body, like a landscape can be codified as primitive, living proof of a backward, premodern time "under the commanding view of the Westerner's eye" (25). Thus, enters the limeña's body in the men's imperialist travel narratives. The sign of the limeña could serve the male travel writer in two ways: on the one hand, her body allowed him a feminine object on which to fix his gaze and generate interest for the reader, much like an Inca ruin; on the other hand, he could criticize her dress in such a way that it would symbolize the neglect of the Peruvian nation. This so-called neglect would, then, persuade one to see the North American or European presence as both benign and necessary because Lima as an unkempt nation would "logically" need its intervening presence.

Regarding this first point, the male subject's gaze is systematic in representing the body as bodyscape: "it procedes systematically from part to part, quantifying and spatializing, noting color and texture and finally passing an aesthetic judgement which stressed the body's role as object to be viewed" (Spurr 23). From the little he can see of her a general complaint of the male travelers which I will examine later the male traveler finds that, on the whole, her body is pleasurable, from her "small, elegantly formed feet" to her "fair face" and "large, bright, dark eyes" (von Tschudi 70).

Yet, after objectifying the woman from viewable body part to body part, her dress requires cultural intervention on a symbolic level; for it is the culprit of the woman's slovenly ways in Peru. After all, as von Tschudi points out the saya y manto allows the limeña from taking the proper "trouble of a careful toilette" (69).

Von Tschudi's comments are in accordance with other male European travel writers. In general, when travel writers engage in discussions of Spanish American society, comments of the Latin American women often appear among textual discussions of the host culture's "filthy habits." The woman, fares poorly in light of the aesthetic judgement of her personal attire and upkeep which simultaneously serves as an unfavorable indictment of the culture she represents. Humboldt, himself, was harsh in his assessment of the limeña. With a curt tone of disappointment and indignation, he writes that he has neither seen ornate houses nor luxuriously dressed women as was rumored. In terms of viewing the limeña, the only thing that stands out for him about her is her habit of cleaning her teeth with a root called raiz de dientes, a custom he deems to be a "horrible spectacle" (Humboldt 78). Though the limeña's body is worth sexualizing, her dress and habits testify in the minds of these male travel writers that she is unkempt. She is mapped as uncivilized territory.

Many male travel writers from imperialist centers are quick to note how difficult it is to really view the tapada with any real assurance that he can be certain of her looks because she is all but concealed by the manto. Writers such as Carleton and von Tschudi are always quick to point out that they can easily mistake an "undesirable" woman for the more sightly limeña. In fact, almost every travelogue I've encountered regarding this topic includes an anecdote about mistaking either an old woman, a blind woman, or a woman of indigenous or African race for what the often racist Anglo and even Creole Peruvian traveler considers the more appealing fair-skinned, Creole limeña to be. Von Tschudi's example readily points out how the gaze can be disappointed, embarrassed or even left frustrated (perhaps even emasculated):

> It is difficult, nay almost impossible, to recognize a lady thus muffled up...On beholding a tall slender figure whose symmetrical contour is discernible...and a bright dark eye beaming beneath the folds of the manto, one may be induced to imagine the charms...concealed beneath...the garb. But how great is the disappointment when an accidental movement of the manto discloses the wide mouth of an ugly mulatta grinning from ear to ear. (von Tschudi 70)

In light of von Tschudi's disappointment and several similar anecdotes that occur in other male travel writers' accounts, we might ask ourselves what happens to the power of the male gaze obstructed, even tricked by the manto. If as Spurr notes, "for the observer, sight confers power; for the observed, visibility is a trap" (Spurr 16), does the tapada deny the male traveler some of his power? Is it the dress that frustrates these male authors (allowing the women to pay less attention to their toilett as they say) or is it the fact that completely viewing these women's faces and bodies is so obstructed that only the feet, the one eye, and the hand are exposed for the pleasure of the male gaze?

Not only is the manto enough to make the male traveler wonder if he, indeed, is sexualizing the right object, but the fact that the limeña is known for her ability to banter with men, to respond to their flirtatious comments, breaks with the notion that the woman remain demure regardless of the amount of attention directed her way. José Victoriano Lastarria, an exiled Chilean who sought refuge and lived many years in Peru, comments on the fact that the tapada not only looks back from behind the protection of her manto but even responds back to any coquettry with a witty tongue. He relates that the tapadas, while seated at a bull-fighting performance, "...ocupan los asientos y están allí como en su estrado recibiendo los dichos, las galanterías y las curiosas manotadas de los transeúntes. Ellas no se inquietan, sino que al contrario charlan y responden con gracia las jovialidades de sus cortejos" (Lastarria 100). In the case described above, the limeña not only looks back, she also responds in kind.

In the case of the women travel writers, their gaze follows the systematic descriptions found in the commanding view used by their male counterparts. The limeña's body is described in a way that increases pleasure. For example, Tristan is just as quick to mention the movements of the limeña's body and how pleasurable her body and walk are for the observer. In the following textual example from Tristan desire escalates with the narration:

> ¡Cuánta gracia tienen, qué embriagadoras son esas bellas limeñas con su saya de un hermoso negro billante al sol...¡Qué graciosos son los movimientos de sus hombros, cuando atraen el manto para ocultar por completo el rostro...¡Qué fino y flexibles es su talle y cuán ondulante es el balanceo de su paso! (218)

The emphasis on the movements ("graciosos") of the limeñas—their manner and sway of walk ("ondulante") suggests that Tristan has incorporated some of the language and focal points so typical of the male gaze. Though with a less sensual diction, Dahlgren writes that "a Limenan señorita, enveloped in manta, the bright eyes alone to be seen, the jewelled hand clasping the folds of the mantle down around her, is always to us attractive and interesting" (39).

For the women travel wirters the limeña also serves as a sign that inspires them as women. Unlike their male compatriats these European and American women writers found the possibility of concealment and the mobility it afforded very desirable. As Pratt has pointed out, "[w]hat other writers record as the uncleanliness and unkemptness of Lima women, Tristan presents as a strategic cultural practice" (Pratt 151). Even Dahlgren, though less adament in championing the rights of women, notes that the Lima woman is completely protected and may go out as she pleases: "...if one wishes to attend an opera, unescorted by a gentlemen, one can do so. Wrapped in the black manta, which quite conceals the features, and accompanied by a maid servant, one is quite protected" (39).

Though these women travel writers do not stress any uncleanliness on the part of the limeña, they are not above writing from an imperial ethos. The gaze of European and North American women writers is split in the sense that the Euro and American women writers envy the limeña's strangely liberated mobility in society; nevertheless, the women travelers are complicit in participating both in the commanding view and in judging the Peruvian culture according to an imperial ethos of cultural superiority. For Tristan and Dahlgren, the limeña is not necessarily unkempt, but rather "out of style," "outdated" and, by association, her country is not modern but behind in the times. Dahlgren writes: "The old national dress of the women, called saya y manto, has disappeared...This change is not to be regretted,...[as nothing, to our eye, can be more ungraceful than the species of straight jacket called saya] the manta is also fast giving way, and must soon be displaced by the modern bonnet" (49). For Dahlgren, the North American bonnet becomes a symbol of progress, an attire the women must emulate to signify their nation's status on the modern timeline. As for Tristan, after first affirming the superior intelligence of the limeña women over their male compatriots, she writes that Peru is still lagging behind according to her scale of civilization:

> La fase de civilización en la que se encuentra este pueblo está aún muy alejada de la que hemos alcanzado en Europa. No existe en el Perú ningún instituto para la educación de uno u otro sexo. La inteligencia no se desarolla sino por sus fuerzas naturales. Por esta causa, la preeminencia de las mujeres de Lima sobre el otro sexo, por inferiores que sean las mujeres europeas con relación a la moral, debe atribuirse a la superioridad de   inteligencia que Dios les ha concedido. (Tristan 220)

Certainly there is a contradiction here, a moment of discursive ambivalence when we consider these European and North American women's assessment of the women they deem to be from less modernized countries: how much liberty is modernity actually granting women on a supposedly universal scale when women from "less modernized, less civilized" societies are granted more freedom in their "backward" and "less modern dress"?

How do the Peruvian nationalists reapropriate the sign of the limeña and imbue her with a signifying quality that talks back to imperialist representations similar to what we have just considered? They uphold her as a site of national patrimony.

Lastarria worries that the limeña in her saya y manto is a national vision that is fading. The following quote from Lastarria's travelogue gives ample indication of the impact of cultural intervention and its erasure of Peruvian signs in the dress of the women. Lastarria laments that the limeña is abandoning her national dress for the European especially the French mode of dress:

> Es verdad que cada día pierde más su poder el bello sexo en Lima, pero la única causa está en que a las señoras les ha dado el capricho de abandonar la saya por el vestido de gros, y el manto por la manteleta y la prosaica gorra de la moda francesa. Ellas conocen que su vestido nacional es más gracioso y más cómodo y que les da más dignidad y libertad; pero culpan de su abandono a sus maridos, que les ordenan vestimenta a la moda europea. (Lastarria 101)

Though they use her sign as a way to talk back and refute those claims and representations made by European and North American travel writers, the Peruvian subjects, also participate in the commanding view, making her a national bodyscape. For example, Fuentes comments on the limeña's sleek body, her small feet and her gait: "El esveltez del cuerpo de las limeñas, lo pequeño y bien formado de sus pies, y la elegancia y desenvoltura de su andar han sido en todo tiempo reconocidos y elojiados" (101).

Nevertheless, sometimes a woman less aesthetically pleasing in Fuentes' view is mistakenly taken for the limeña por excelencia. Thus enters the anecdote of being horrified by the disclosure of an undesirable, older and toothless woman: "Un elegante cuerpo, un blanco y torneado brazo, un ligero y pequeño pie, un pedazito de ojo negro y expresivo, solían pertenecer a una abuela desmolada" (102).

Though like his European and American contemporaries, Fuentes is quick to mention the fact that the limeña's dress conceals the woman's identity or, in fact, deceives the viewer, the dress or attire in no way indicates slovenly nature of the nation on a symbolic level. Quite the contrary, the limeña in her saya y manto serves as a symbol of beauty and grace of national proportion. In fact, we find Fuentes' narration of the limeña's dress under the heading "Vestidos nacionales" (101).

For Fuentes, the limeña not only attests to the civilized and graceful culture of the autonomous Peruvian nation, but he also reminds the readers that those Peruvians considered best to represent the nation are the fairer-skinned, the Creoles exemplified by the limeña because she is often lighter-skinned than the Creole male. According to Fuentes, "El color de los limeños...es trigueño, pálido y amarilloso, siendo mucho más blanco el de las mujeres" (101).

The sign of the limeña changes from representation to representation depending on from what locus of enunciation the travel writer produces his/her text. Personal, social, economic and political agendas dress her differently. For the imperialist male travel writers, her body is desirable yet her toilett warants disdain; to the proto/feminist women travel writers, the limeña is simultaneously liberated and outdated; yet for the cosmopolitan male Peruvian writers, the limeña is a testament to national patrimony and national autonomy. Under the guise of saya y manto a nation's representation is at stake.

For the Creole—and Mestizo in the case of Bustamante to try to dispute notions of his intellectually (and even physically) inferior status, he must enter the debate representing Peru as a nation not behind in the evolutionary timeline of those Western nations having reached a so-called state of progress which brings up the use of stereotyping others to ensure and elevate the subject's authority. Like their imperialist counterparts, the Peruvian travel writers engaged in this rhetorical strategy due to their dilemma as subjects from a supposed "backward nation" how must they authorize themselves to represent their fellow Peruvians?

As examined in chapter two, imperialist subjects often elevate their superiority through their "superior" race, further elevated through "superior" cultural traits contrasted to those cultural and racial traits they find in the Peruvian population. One should not be surprised then that the Peruvian travelers engage in this same form of racist mapping. However, the context behind such a need to assert racial superiority for the Creole intellectual over national others is different.

In chapter two, we examined how imperialist writers engaged in very racist caricatures especially in regards to the Afro-Peruvian and the indigenous peoples of Peru. However, the Creole population was not immune to characterizations of inherent inferiority. At some point in their texts, all the imperialist travelers under consideration for this project insert indictments against the Creoles—either characterizing them as "indolent" or "poorly educated" or "lacking refined taste." Of these writers, von Tschudi is the most damning: "They shrink from anything that demands intellectual exertion. In short, they are sworn enemies to business of every kind...The intellectual culture of the white Creole of Lima is exceedingly defective...I have often been amazed at the monstrous ignorance of the so-called educated Peruvians" (66). Von Tschudi is willing to admit that he has come into contact with some notable Peruvian scholars. Nevertheless, he qualifies any exceptions with the disclamatory statement before commencing his detailed classification of races and Peruvian types: "I have met with some honorable exceptions; though, unfortunately, they were mere solitary luminaries, whose transient light has been speedily obscured by the surrounding darkness" (67). In other words, exceptions are aberrant and easily bracketted off from those Peruvian Creoles he characterizes in aggregate, exemplifying for him an overlying, constructed "truth"—the Creoles mirror the inefficiency and incompetence found in the Peruvian nation.

For the Creole writing subject to dispel imperialist notions of his intellectual (and even physical) inferiority, he must enter the debate representing Peru as a nation not behind in the evolutionary timeline. In doing so, he must put himself in the top rung of national subjects, authorizing himself as a knowledgeable, active Peruvian subject, distanced from those Peruvians "marked" as objects obviously "other" and "less civilized," i.e. Peru's indigenous and African populations, racialized designations inhereted from a racist and colonial ideology.[13] This racist mode of "othering" is a message emitted into two directions: a) to refute imperialist representations of the Creole's "inherent inferiority"; and b) to convince the Peruvian people that those best suited to guide Peru are those belonging to the Creole race.

Though perhaps not allotting the same breadth of textual space to racializing others as do their imperialist counterparts, the Peruvian writers do, indeed, participate in this convention but with a different motive. Their agenda is to construct national "others" supposedly "less civilized" and, by extention, "less capable" of guiding Peru into a more progressive present. Their use of racializing others allows them to create a hierarchy that differs little in theory from the racial mapping that occurs in the discourses of foreign travelers to Peru. However, the purpose is manipulated into another direction: to authorize a certain class and race as "naturally superior," and, therefore, the more legitimate nationals left to govern the nation are those who correspond to an elite more resembling the Creole Peruvians.

I say "resembling" because race and class can work together in ways that allow a writing subject like Bustamante, a Mestizo whose mother was supposedly a descendent of Tupac Amaru, to participate in a similar fashion.[14] Though Bustamante was often a defender of Andean indigenous rights, criticizing, for example, the government for taking in Quechua soldiers into their armies without employing Quechau-speaking commanders (Bustamante 36-37); his class allowed him certain opportunities. Thus, he had become a world-reknowned traveler known as "el Inca" and was offered a postion as a traveling "diputado" due to his ability to speak Quechua. It was his responsibility to examine the departments of Ayacucho, Huancavelica and Junín—for the first time under the young Republic of Peru. Bustamante had reached a level of respect and stature that afforded him the ability to speak from an "enlightened" position over his "purely" indigenous others. For example, while bemoaning how priests often mistreated Quechua laborers working on the church-owned chacras, he, nevertheless, refers to the indigenous workers as "criaturas casi salvajes" (35).

Valdéz y Palacios shows less sympathy than does Bustamante especially concerning indigenous tribes found in the jungled regions of Peru. Part of Valdéz y Palacios itinerary takes him to a region he considers little civilized because neither the Inca reign of the Spanish administration sought to populate and administer the region, leaving it abandoned to its own "savage" tribes and tribal customs (Valdéz y Palacios 97). There exists, however, La Misión de Cocabambilla, which serves as a meeting ground and the site of a week-long market that brings together several "tribus salvajes," Valdéz and Palacios' reference to the Antis and the Chontaquiros. All the signifiers used to mark the "savages" that appear in this section are easily discernible to those who study colonial discourse: the exotic native dress by day contrasted to the nudity of their bodies by night, the enslaved tribal women, the mannerisms that are almost chaotic in their energy.

Valdéz y Palacios is especially memsmerized by the greeting calls, the sound and movement these people demonstrate either while greeting or celebrating with one another from their "gritos de júbilo" to their "movimiento eléctrico"; "muévense y se agitan en todas las direcciones con una alegría imponderable" (99). They engage in "himnos salvajes," sport "adornos selváticos" and "encienden grandes fogatas, hacen su cena y después se echan a dormir, desnudos sobre la arena y al lado del fuego" (100). They are a curiosity to witness, signifying at every moment their "otherness" while the writing subject remains a civilized "forastero" by contrast, observing their activities.

Fuentes' text offers plenty of racist stereotypes as well. Whereas Valdéz y Palacios engages in racist rhetoric towards the "salvajes" of the jungled regions in Peru, Fuentes' racism against indigenous peoples is abundant when describing the Andean Indians. Take, for example, his description of the india serrana that serves as a great contrast to his laudatory remarks about the limeña: "La india serrana no es ni muy activa ni muy inteligente y con dificultad llega á hablar bien el castellano" (Fuentes 94). His remarks concerning the limeña not only praise the color of her skin—"siendo mucho mas blanco" than that of her male counterparts—but also her traits of "inteligencia y de imaginacion tanto mas notables cuanto que la educacion femenina ha estado, hasta ahora pocos años, casi totalmente descuidada...Las mujeres tienen, en genral, pronta comprension..." (100).

When describing the indios serranos that make up part of the Peruvian infantry, he describes them as "indolent" and attributes their proclivity to deserting the forces to their constant play of their native musical form, the yaraví:

> El flautin se presta mucho á la música melancólica y sentimental que caracteriza al yarabí, cancion indígena del Perú, con que el habitante de la sierra expresa sus dolores y su amor...Pocos son los indios que no tocan el flautín, oye el soldado los tristes gemidos que el instrumento lanza y...se apodera de su corazon la melancolía, y deserta de las filas para regresar á su cabaña. (174)

According to Fuentes, the only remedy to this problem of desertion is to prohibit that any soldier be allowed to have the instrument to play such music that encourages indolence (174).

Up to this point, the refashioning of tropes that the Peruvian writers employ serve more so than not to refute imperialist representations that denigrate Peru's status. However, regarding the Peruvian subjects inventory of Peru's natural resources and sites of Inca splendor, especially in the texts of Valdéz y Palacios and Bustamante, the message is not crafted solely to talk back to imperialist centers, but to peak Peruvians' interest in their own national affairs. Whereas regarding national customs, the Peruvian writers launch their message more toward imperialist notions that other Peru as uncivilized, when discussing the landscape of Peru, the message appears to turn more toward a Peruvian readership to rally Peruvians to represent themselves. This is not to say that messages weren't multidirectional regarding representing the Peruvians subjects' discussion of customs and race. However, the address toward fellow Peruvians becomes more audible when the inventory of resources and ruins takes place.

Like the travelogues of the early explorers to Latin America, the abundance found in the Peruvian landscape takes on a paradiscal quality. This is especially notable in Valdéz y Palacios' text. This quality is reminiscent of Pratt's consideration of how Creoles refashioned the wonderous abundance theme in which an inventory points out the paradaisacal fecundity of the land.[15] Though Pratt's study centered around the poetry of Andrés Bello, we find a similar rhetoric here in Valdéz y Palacios' travelogue. With a brief comment that preceeds his description of the lands that comprise the "quebradas de Calca, Taray y Urubamaba," Valdéz y Palacios immediately sets up the region as un "paraíso terrenal" (25). There he finds "delicious gardens" fortified by the "abundant" "fertilizing waters" of the Vilcamayo River with pictoresque villas nearby as well "otros poblados de bosques y de airosas y verdes arboledas" with "infinitvos torrentes de agua cristalina" (26). One finds in his travelogue constant reminders of the Sierra's region offering worthy advantages everywhere: in San Salvador one finds hard-working people dedicated "todos a la labranza y comercio; in Pisac one encounters a variety of foodstuffs celebrated "por su rica carne, sus quesos, mantequilla y patatas que hay allí en abundancia" ; in Coya one can even expect to increase his/her longevity due to a lovely climate allowing people to live to be 90 or 100 years old (41-43).[16]

Valdéz y Palacios maximizes the beauty of the Andes and equates their majestic quality as rivals to the more famous mountain ranges found in Europe. The comparison inserts Peru in the ranks of other nations, yet toys with the idea that the Andes exceed the beauty of European ranges:

> América está virgen y ún no está vista por los europeos en sus lugares más bellos y misteriosos. Esto no es de extrañar: sus mismos hijos acostumbrados a sus encantos desde que nacen, ya no reciben las impresiones que ella produce...Las campiñas de Urubamba, tal vez más bellas que aquéllas [de Suiza e Italia], sólo necesitan un bardo inspirado para atraer sobre ellas las miradas del mundo. (Valdéz y Palacios 53)

One notes that it is not the populousness that impresses these writers so much as the resources and vigor of the inhabitants themselves. Whereas small towns are easily dismissed by the imperialist travel writers and signify a lack of development, descriptions of such small communities do not yield the same tone of negativity in the texts of Valdéz y Palacios and Bustamante; it is the surroundings and the character of the people that impresses, not the size of the town. Regardless of any town's size, each town offers some valuable resource and splendor: "Cada una de estas poblaciones tiene un encanto particular que sería largo describir; pero tienen tambien ciertos aspectos de belleza que son comunes a todos," "lindas casas," "una vegetación frondosa," and "bellos jardines" (Valdéz y Palacios 43).

The issue of talking back to imperialists is not so confrontational as to sever altogether any future trade relations. The idea was more to insure fairer practices and secure respect. The desire was one that would survive a delicate balance between good world commerce without losing Peru's status as an autonomous nation in charge of its own progress. For example, Valdéz y Palacios frequently bemoans the fact that the European imagination remains oblivious to the beauty and literary potential of Andean countrysides and landscapes. Representing towns and natural settings near Urubamba, the subject talks back to the blank space in the literary imagination of Euorpean writers: "Este es otro lugar pintoresco que la imaginación de los novelistas europeos no ha adivinado aún" (29).

Though all three of the Peruvian nationalists talk back in one way or another to imperialist representations of Peru, the travelogues of Bustamante (from the department of Puno) and Valdéz y Palacios (from the department of Cuzco) point out another center at which to direct criticism: Lima. Both subjects exhibit certain indignation at how the Lima and coastal nationals were attempting to construct a national hegemony that would leave out their Serrano compatriots. However, rather than split these writers off in terms of regional allegiances, examining the political context of the period shows that such a dichotomy goes against the ambivalent and complex nature of such allegiances based exclusively on regions.

Before looking at how Serrano voices talk back through the two travelogues looked at for this chapter, a certain foregrounding of early republican strains of political thought needs to be addressed. The first three quarters of nineteenth century Peru makes pointing dichotomous political parties impossible since there are not concrete divisions to identify into neat categories. Republican nationalist lines of discourses were affected not only by conservative versus liberal thought but rather filtered through additional veins: regional alliances, class and ethnic lines. Many centers involving port or Andean cities were vying for becoming the national center: Lima, Cuzco, Callao and Arequipa – the two strongest contenders among them being Lima and Cuzco.

These convoluted lines of political discourses match the vacillating state of Peru—varying economic policies and inconstant governmental regimes complicated by caudillo politics . Only President Gamarra actually completed a four-year term until the presidency of Ramón Castilla in 1844. However, as Charles Walker points out, in addition to divisions between ethnic and social groups, one of the most prominent regional divisions that undercut Peru was the one existing "between Lima and the Southern Andes" (Walker 85).

Since, as Benedict Anderson puts it, "'nationalism'...invents nations where they do not exist," in early republican Peru instead of national hegemonies having firm footholds in the nation's politics precarious still-forming national polities were involved in the constant fashioning of national community (6). Though limeño Creole elites and Mestizo and/or Creole Serranos embarked on different national imaginings they did share a historical descent, to some extent a mobilized desire to fight imperialist exploitation and a desire for the formation of a Peru that would garner and push for cultural and economic respect from imperialist nations ever-eyeing their national resources.

This understanding allows for some acceptance of the ambivalence in national discourse or national community imaginings: "...regardless of the actual inequality and exploitation that may prevail in each [imagined community], the nation is always conceived as a deep, horizontal comradeship" (7).

All three writers were, indeed, republicans. However, the first half of the century involved varying degrees of liberalism and conservativism among Peruvian intellectuals and politicians alike. On the whole, conservative republicans hailed a more centralist government with more protectionist policies rather than a complete policy of comercio libre which liberals were more apt to hail.

Neither liberals nor conservatives had a stronghold in either Southern or Northern Peru but had an often wavering following in both regions which hints at another factor that complicated political allegiances: Lima/coastal politicians, whether liberal or conservative, sought to post the central government in Lima to the chagrin of their Serrano compatriots. If one can be sure of one antagonistic factor, it's that the majority of southern Peruvians shared a "long-standing distaste for Lima centralism" (149). Several researchers studying this period—Nils Jacobsen, Charles Walker, Mark Thurner and Heraclio Bonilla, among them point to a long tradition of Creole liberals exacerbating this conflict, either abandoning, denigrating or simply being incognizant of the Andean regions. E. de Sartiges, a French traveler, who traveled through Peru during the same period that Flora Tristan did, offers us an example of this rivalry between costeños and serranos. He shows the attitudes that pitted Serrano and coastal cultures against one another:

> Los serranos dicen que los limeños y los arequipeños son espíritus ligeros, que reniegan de sus costumbres nacionales para adoptar sin comprenderlas y copiar falsamente las costumbres de los extranjeros. Los otros tratan a los serranos de gente ruda e insociable...Se burlan sobre todo de su manera de arrastrar las palabras al hablar y de las numerosas expresiones familiares que no reconoce el castellano puro hablado en las ciudades de la costa. (de Sartiges 68)[17]

Bustamante and Valdéz y Palacios write neither from a clearly liberal nor conservative position. Both tend toward a protectionist desire for the textile and agricultural markets in southern Peru. However, especially in the case of Bustamante, the ideal citizen—including an indigenous citizen would achieve such superior status through a modern and enlightened mode of living which tends toward a more liberal discourse (Jacobsen 145).[18]

What remains clear in both writers, however, is their indignation against the Lima elite, conservative or not, which they felt either totally ignored southern Peru or held it in contempt. This is not a surprising point since both authors wrote and published their writings during the 1840s after the termination of General Agustín Gamarra's second term as president. Gamarra's platform (during his first term from 1829-1833 and his second term during 1838-1841) called for protectionist policies especially of Peru's textile industry in southern Peru and centralizing the government in Cuzco. But during the presidency of Castilla lasting from 1844-1868, Limeñan liberals initially supported Castilla and the national center reverted back to Lima:

> Generally considered a watershed event in modern Peruvian history, Castilla's 'liberal revolution' signaled Lima's midcentury sea change toward the free-trade liberalism...As the modernizing coastal elite prospered...the opulent 'Lima State' would drift away from the interior highland regions. (Thurner 45)

Another factor solidifying this focus on Lima and the coastal region was the burgeoning guano market which began in the late 1840s, peaking during the 1850s and 60s. As Jacobsen finds in his investigation of the Cuzco region, "[a]fter 1840 the relative importance of the city [of Cuzco] and region declined" (229). The sierra region had lost its prominence much to the dismay of Bustamante and Valdéz y Palacios, which is enunciated in their travelogues in a number of instances that affirms a Serrano protest.

Even the Serranos' travel itinerary, national mapping and geographical inventory breaks convention with itineraries normally taken by travel writers in Peru and suggests an assertion of Andean voices not heard before and highlight a resistance to limiting representations of Peru based on travels that confined themselves primarily to the region around Lima. Whereas Valdéz y Palacios begins his travelogue in Cuzco, Bustamante does so in Puno. These new, noncanonical itineraries open up new areas to applaud, new realms of abundance to uncover and new financial potential to expose. Generally for the foreign traveler, the typical itinerary through Peru involved arriving at Callao; from Callao going on to Lima; then, perhaps, Arequipa and Santa Rosa which were often farewell stops to Peru en route to Chile.[19] However, Cuzco, and especially Puno, were scarcely considered necessary stopping points unless the travelers were traveling archeologists interested in the Inca ruins such as Von Tschudi.[20]

With the laudatory remarks about the Andean regions, both Valdéz y Palacios and Bustamante lampoon the country's mismanagement, or even total ignorance, of the Altiplano's potential for commerce which allowed other nations to usurp Peruvians' own potential wealth and status in the global market of the period. For example, Bustamante interrogatively laments:

> ¿Estaremos condenados a vegetar entre tesoros e ignorancia dejando inocentemente los primeros para que sean presa de extranjeros codiciosos, que vuelven enriquecidos a sus respectivos países para desde allí echarnos en cara con imprudente ingratitud

nuestra sandez, nuestra indolencia, y hasta la franca hospitalidad con que los acogemos? (Bustamante 27)

The quote above exemplifies a double discourse that talks back to and berates several centers of power—imperialist nations who usurp Peru's natural resources and Peru's government whose allegiance to Lima diverts attention and protection away from one if its own national regions: the Sierra. As Bustamante puts it, Peru is not governing in a manner that is "eminentemente nacional":

> Si de veras deseamos que el país sea grdande y respetado, atendamos de una vez a los medios que le pueden conducir a su engrandecimiento...sin duda para mayor dicha de la que hoy disfrutan sus hijos que son desgraciados no más que por falta de una administración inteligente, juiciosa, y llena de un espíritu eminentemente nacional. (Bustamante 27-28)

Complaints charging neglect of the area by the government comes across most directly when the serrano writers catalogue the crops in the region that signify originality and that have not been capitalized fully by the nation. Some crops that both Bustamante and Valdéz y Palacios discuss are the region's yield of cameloid wool, cacao and coca all of which signify great potential if the Peruvian administration would turn its attention to the sierra.

Though many scholars point out that imperialist nations had great interest in the coastal region's guano reserves, Nils Jacobson reminds us that the demand for woolen products, especially in England, garnered a great deal of interest in Peru's wool, especially the alpaca wool. Originally, the market of woolen textiles extended to all regions of the country, but when Peru began exporting raw wool to England, the Peruvian elite, especially the elite on the coast, began buying English goods, manufactured from Peruvian wool. The elite began to scoff at Peruvian textiles in favor of English and other European tailored products. Peru's wool market turned from producing goods for all sectors of Peruvian consumption to producing raw resources for European markets that then furnished tailored goods as imports that the elite coastal Peruvians purchased (Jacobsen 52).[21] Bustamante laments at how Andean woven goods are scoffed at by Peru's own citizens: "Hay en Cuzco fábricas de tejidos pero va en una decadencia notable...mal que se atribuye...al desuso o desprecio que tienen a ese tejido los mismos hijos del país, pareciéndoles demasiado ordinario" (Bustamante 43). He then asserts that it is the government's responsibility to encourage the industry and those who would ignore Peruvian style and goods for those manufactured in European markets:

¿No es, en efecto, obligación del gobierno el estímulo de la industria del país...? ¿Por qué vestir a nuestros soldados de paños europeos maleados, todos ellos endebles, y sin más en su abono que el buen parecer exterior?...¡Qué ramo de riqueza escondido en esos veinte mil quintales de lana...que anualmente nos lleva el extranjero por un precio vil, para   vendérnoslos luego...! Es decir que sobre esa pérdida en nuestros propios intereses, todavía se nos sigue la ruina de nuestras fábricas...para los goces y el engrandecimiento de la industria europea. (44)

Both Valdéz y Palacios and Bustamante inventory crops ignored for its potential value: cacao and coca. Bustamante finds as much potential in the chocolate industry as he does in the woolen textile industry, but the outside world is unaware of its worth: "La excelencia del cacao del Cuzco no es conocida en la Europa, y es un mal para el país que le produce, mal de que también hay que acusar a nuestro gobierno pues debiera atender a que ese artículo de tanto consumo se diera a conocer en los mercados europeos" (43). Valdéz y Palacios shares this frustration of the cacao's potential not just being unknown to European markets but being ignored by Lima consumers: "...[N]o se exporta para el extranjero sino muy raras veces y en pequeñas cantidades. La misma capital de Lima no recibe sino pequeñas cantidades, a pesar del gusto que tienen los limeños por el chocolate, y del valor que le dan en esa capital..." (Valdéz y Palacios 90).

Coca is another native and therefore original crop for these subjects to underscore for a national product to export for the betterment of Peru's economy. Both Bustamante and Valdéz y Palacios highlight yerba de coca's healthful benefits. Though Bustamante warns not using it in excess, he nevertheless applauds its "virtud alimenticia y confortativa" (Bustamante 42). Valdéz y Palacios goes even further, stressing that as a tea it rivals even English teas, surpassing it due to it being devoid of stimulants, and verifies it with anecdotal evidence: "Más de una vez se ha hecho el experimento de darlo a los ingleses, que son sin duda los mejores conocedores de té que hay, y lo han tomado por té perla (así en el original) con la mayor buena fe" (Valdéz y Palacios 89).

Valdéz y Palacios admits, coca is not indigenous only to Peru but to Bolivia as well. However, what sets Peru's wealth in coca apart from Bolivia's is that the coca in Bolivia is "de calidad inferior" (89). It's a native crop distinct even from Bolivia's and Valdéz y Palacios decries that Peru is not taking advantage of it as a resource of its very own:

Si bajo un govierno establecido se hubiese desenvuelto el espíritu de industria en el Perú y los hijos de este país se hubieran dedicado a buscar en los productos de su suelo...se converitría la coca en género de vasta exportación para el extranjero y habría sido un manantial inagotable de riqueza para este país. (88-89)

This urgent call to develop Peru's own national foodstuffs for a world market takes on even more significance if we remember, as was pointed out in chapter two, that European travelers were scouting out Peru's soil to insert and harvest Western European foodstuffs. Von Tschudi's travelogue offers us an excellent example in which his agricultural gaze posits itself in the Sierra readying Peru's fertile ground for European fruit trees: "Cherries, plums, and chestnuts I did not see in Peru, yet I believe the climate of Sierra is very favorable to their growth" (von Tschudi 130).

Besides the ignorance of crops, these Serrano subjects also bemoan the ignorance of the literary wealth that could be procured by finding inspiration in the Andean landscape and Andean ruins. Bustamante points out that only foreign travelers seem to be cataloguing and representing Andean ruins. After viewing an Inca monument, Intihuatana found in the Cuzqueñan region, Bustamante writes about how, upon returning to his inn, he finds members of the national guard posted nearby. Bustamante decides to ask them about the ruins: "¿Han visto Uds. ese monumento? Les pregunté yo, a lo que me respondieron con admirable gravedad: No pero el general Bolívar ha subido a verla, y otros muchos caballeros muy distinguidos, sin contar con los extranjeros que también se han tomado la misma molestia" (48). Bustamante is clearly disappointed at their response: "¿No es más que ridículo el que los hijos del mismo país, donde esas reliquias...existen, nada sepan de ella sino es lo que le dicen los curiosos que viajan por allí?" (48).

Such disappointment corresponds to a predicament in which nations like Mexico and various Andean nations found themselves: travelers of the period interested in indigenous archeology of the Aztecs, Mayas and Incas were claiming greater knowledge over Amerindian cultures and authorizing themselves over local authorities, citing that the local inhabitants had no interest in them. Quoting Stephen Greenblatt, David Johnson discusses how travelers of the period engaged ina "rhetoric of wonder" which facilitated the 'renaming, transformation and appropriation' of another cultures ruins. Hence, the urgency in Bustamante's tone is well warranted given the period.[22]

Very real to Bustamante's concern is a primary example of how Europeans were claiming superior knowledge over Inca ruins, culture and history. Historians of Inca civilization were entering a debate trying to date the length of time Inca civilization actually existed. Bustamante, upon describing all the ruins and sites of interest in the city of Cuzco, attempts to correct historians who were undercuting the period during which the Inca empire existed:

> Todos esos monumentos son testimonios inequívocos de que los antiguos moradores de nuestro país, no desconocieron la civilización ni las artes y en vano se empeñan los

historiadores en queren [sic] persuadirnos de que la existencia de los Incas no fue de larga duración. (24)

One historian Bustamante might well be responding back to is William H. Prescott whose History of the Conquest of Peru (published a few years before Bustamante's text) was often cited as the authority on Inca history. Prescott is one such historian that was refuting that the duration of the Inca empire could well exceed 400 years before the arrival of the Spaniard's: "The date usually assigned for these extraordinary events was about four hundred years before the coming of the Spaniards...But, however pleasing to the imagination, and however popular, the legend of Manco Capac, it requires but little reflection to show its improbability..." (Prescott 32). Prescott then goes on to disprove that figure with his own "little reflection":

> No account assigns to the Inca dynasty more than thirteen princes before the Conquest. But this number is altogether too small to have spread over four hundred years, and would not carry back the foundations of the monarchy, on any probable computation, beyond two centuries and a half - an antiquit not incredible in itself...The fiction of Manco Capac and his sister-wife was devised, no doubt, at a later period, to gratify the vanity of the Peruvian monarchs. (33)

Just as Fuente's had talked back to the likes of foreign travelers who would denigratingly misrepresent Peru, Bustamante tackles the historians who would try authorize themselves as sole authorities on Inca history. Though Prescott's correction of the time-span of the Inca dynasty holds true, what is important here is that Bustamante still asserts a voice of resistance.

Valdéz y Palacios is actually concerned about how niether Peruvians nor their European contemporaries find literary inspiration in the sierra regions of Peru. The Andes remain a site of literary absence:

> América está virgen y aún no está vista por los eruopeos en sus lugares más bellos y misteriosos. Esto no es de extrañar: sus mismos hijos acostumbrados a sus encantos desde que nacen, ya no reciben las impresiones que ella produce...Las campiñas de Urubamba, tal vez más bellas que aquellas [de Suiza o Italia], sólo necesitan un bardo inspirado para atraer sobre ellas las miradas del mundo...Es éste un cuadro que, más que al viajero, pertenece al poeta y al escritor. (Valdéz y Palacios 54)

This attempt to include the Sierra regions of the country into the national landscape and to garner the respect it deserves from European and Peruvian eyes alike is especially apparent in the following quote from Valdéz y Palacios.

> Seguramente la vida humana es la misma en cualquier país con poca diferencia...En todo el universo es el mismo lenguage de los ojos que habla por instinto a la juventud y que la vejez dicen que olvida. En el verano, a las ocho de la tarde lo hablan desde Pekín hasta Roma, en el Capitolio y en Constantinopla, en el prado de Madrid...en los Campos Elíseos de París, ...en la Alameda de Lima, en el Lago do Paço de Río de Janeiro; pero en ningún lugar es ciertamente tan expresivo como en la calle del puente de Urubamba. (53)

Valdéz y Palacios incorporates Lima on a par with other world centers on the one hand, but then elevates the Urubamban region above other worldy centers and even above Lima itself. It is clear that these writers feel slighted by imperialist and Limeñan nationalists alike.

In summary, all three Peruvian writers respond back to imperialist representations of Peruvian society through a refashioning of signs imperialist writers used themselves to invalidate the nascent Peruvian nation. If we consider Homi Bhabha's assertion that within the juncture of the act of enunciation and it's product, the content uttered, there is a "third space" of rupture, we can note the futile fixity of signs with which imperialist writers worked so hard to fix Peru and its inhabitants as "backward" and in need of cultural, political and economic intervention. Housed in this third space of enunciation is a site in which "the discursive conditions of enunciation...insure that the meaning and symbols of culture have no primordial unity or fixity; that even the same signs can be appropriated, translated, rehistoricized anew" (Bhabha 37). Thanks to that third space that exposes the precariousness in the imperialist discourse, the discourses of these Peruvian subjects expose the falsehood of any imperialist "transparency" and intercede, appropriating some of the same signs of imperialist travel writing to accent them for decidedly different national agendas. In the case of the Serrano writers such reappropriated signs talk back to various centers— any center which would ignore them, forget them or denigrate them, Peruvian or otherwise. Their need to represent Peru becomes doubly important: not only do they have to talk back to imperialist notions of Peru as an "inferior" culture; they also have to speak up to centralist Lima nationals who would exclude them in a developing national imaginary.

Notes

1. This refers to Graham Robert's explanation of heteroglossia in *The Bakhtin Reader*, edited by Pam Morris.

2. See Pratt's chapter entitled, "Reinventing América/Reinventing Europe: Creole Self-fashioning."

3. We can see this connection in Bustamante's travelogue. In the commencement of his first chapter under the section, "La América," he writes about what produces certain pleasure for him while traveling: "Si es verdad que la naturaleza pone en cada uno de los seres el sello de una inclinación particular...el aspecto característico de la mía se manifiesta...en una muy pronunciada pasión por andar corriendo el mundo de un extremo a otro, para ver y observar los usos y costumbres de tantos y tan diferentes pueblos...(17).

4. See Spurr's chapter "Surveillance: Under Wester Eyes" and Pratt's chapter "Science, planetary con-sciousness, interiors."

5. See Franco's chapter, "Literature and Nationalism," Cornejo Polar's article, "Relaciones entre el costumbrismo peruano y el español" and Brushwood's chapter, "Major Movements and Spanish-American Variations."

6. In terms of *costumbrismo*, John Brushwood has pointed out that its vein of realism should be understood in terms of its mimetic quality (Brushwood 4).

7. Campbell's definition of a monomyth is a basic narrative repeated in various cultures though the trappings around the plot might differ; a monomyth is "the one shape-shifting yet marvelously constant story" (Campbell 3).

8. Deborah Poole has identified the writer that Fuentes is alluding to as the travel writer Viscount Laurent Saint-Cricq, who used the pseudonym of Paul Marcoy (*Vision* 231).

9. Pratt also discusses this problematic of Creole identity (Pratt 112-113).

10. In addition to Chatterjee, see also Mauricio Tenorio Trillo's, "Essaying the History of National Images" (60).

11. A few paragraphs later, she equates the behavior of the spectators at a mystery play to what she imagines she would find in the Middle Ages due to the people's "brutalidad" as well as their "extrema y estúpida superstición" (214).

12. As we will find later in the chapter, this Sierra-centered version of the *yaravi* is strikingly different than the one we will find in Fuentes's version.

13. Several postcolonialists have examined this ideological inheritance. Among them are Homi Bhabha, David Spurr, Bill Ashcroft, Gareth Griffiths, and Helen Tiffin.

14. This line of decendency is supported by Belisario Soto cited in Ricardo Arbulú Vargas' "Juan Bustamante, 1808-1868" (9).

15. See Pratt (172-174).

16. Though Bustamante does not play with the theme of abundance as overtly as Valdéz y Palacios, one does find it ocassionaly in the text while he's offering an inventory of resources and crops in various departments. It is while he describes his native department, Puno, and home town, Vilque, that the tone of paradaisical abundance is most noticeable: "[E]l departamento a que yo pertenezco mantiene mucho ganado lanar, y sus pampas, formando horizonte, abundan en pastos en exquisitos terrenos que se llaman *ahijaderos* o *moyas*" (Bustamante 31; author's emphasis).

17. If one remembers previously in this chapter about how Peruvian writers also engage in rascist representations of national "others," one will find that this quote sheds light on how Fuente's version of *la india serrana* used the signifier of language, *castellano puro*, to emphasis the *serrana's* supposed lack of intelligence.

18. Thurner also sees this as fitting under the "enlightened liberal ideal" (Thurner 5).

19. Some examples of this include Madeleine Dahlgren's *South Sea Sketches* (1881); Karl Scherzer's *Visit to Peru* (1859); Mrs. Howard Vincent's *From China to Peru* (1894); George Carleton's *Our Artist in Peru* (1866); and Ida Pfeiffer's *A Lady's Second JourneyAround the World* (1856). Though Charles Brand did travel to some ruins in southern Peru, he primarily clung to the coast. Any mention of Cuzco in his *Journal of a Voyage to Peru* (1828) pertains only to what roads might lead a potential traveler to Cuzco.

20. See Clements R. Markham's *Cuzco: A Journey to the Ancient Capital of Peru* (1856) and E. George Squier's *Peru: Incidents of Travel and Exploration in the Land of the Incas* (1877). Whereas Squier does, indeed, go to Puno, primarily as a stop on his way to the ruins at Sillustani, his comments about Puno the city as well as Puno the department are minimal. In fact, he dedicates only two paragraphs to a description of Puno, finding it "a dreary place" (357). The subtitle to his Chapter XVIII is telling, not only, of Squier's attitude

toward Puno, but apparently of an attitude shared by travelers in general: "Detour to Puno." E. de Sartiges, likewise, stops over in Puno on his way to Sillustani but dedicates his chapter on Puno only to mining techniques in his *Viaje a las Repúblicas de América del Sur* (1834). His two paragraphs of description of Puno are minimal and match his most pejorative conclusion: "No hay sociedad alguna en Puno..." (31).

21. Jacobson reminds us that though the Creole, Mestizo and elite manufactures turned away from textile production, it did, nevertheless, continue at the peasant level: "With the withdrawl of creole and mestizo manufacturers and merchants from textile production, an increasing share of the raw wool...stayed in control of peasants for processing, subsistence consumption and barter and trade" (Jacobsen 56).

22. Probably the two most notable traveling archeaologists to Peru during this period are Squier and Markham. Von Tschudi was also a well-known archeologist during the period but has received miniscule attention to date in postcolonial studies.

• CHAPTER FIVE •

Conclusion

Upon my initial review of scholarship published on travel writing in the nineteenth century and while I was preparing to write this book, I found ample research about imperialist travel writers in general, though they concerned imperialist travel texts pertaining primarily to Africa and Asia. Some research has been directed more recently toward studying imperialist travelers to Latin America. Still, few studies exist that concentrate on such travelogues concerning Peru more specifically. That studies are scant concerning travel narratives about Peru specifically is surprising, since Peru garnered the attention of many expansionist designs since the Spanish conquest of Peru and during the Age of Guano.

This oversight in the field leaves gaps open in terms of what travel writing conventions look like when specifically involving the site of Peru. Though Pratt and others point out the two most often mentioned sights, that of the tapada, and that of the miscegenated population, there are a multitude of other and other-ed must-sees. Among them are the bullfights, the tambos, the gallinazos, the religious processions, and the Inca roadways and ruins – as Ghosts in the Machine underscores in relation to prescribed travel itineraries and ideological itineraries. Often researchers examine nineteenth-century travel narratives by analyzing only one grouping of writers: either imperialist male writers; or exclusively women writers from Europe and the U.S.; or Latin American writers who wrote about their travels abroad to Europe and the United States. This tendency produces studies limited in terms of looking at the multiple participants in the dialogue concerning post-independent Latin America and/or Peru. For example, as we saw in Constructing Peru: Imperialist Representations of a Backward Nation, women writers often share some of the very same tropes of othering as men travelers do. In the cases of Tristan and Dahlgren, each demonstrated a proclivity to suggest how her country could tap into markets not considered by her country's trade policies. They also produced their own informal inventories of Peru's natural resources. Likewise they attend many of the same nodal points of sights and sites on their travel itineraries which serve the ideological underpinnings of their ideological itineraries. This tendency to bracket women travelers in a category of their own and apart from the writings of the Capitalist Vanguard obscures their involvement in supporting and fortifying imperialist agendas (Pratt 146-155).

Women travelers do offer some narrative differences, however, in the sense that they inject gender in their texts as well as use their narratives to champion more rights for women. This is especially the case in regards to how they maternalize the travel convention of the danger motiff. Comparing men and women's travelogues alongside one another allows one to examine how women writers are equally complicit as willing purveyors of imperialist ideology while simultaneously manipulating the genre to express their personal desires to be allowed more political involvement in nationalist issues.

Perhaps the most misleading effect of excluding certain groups who were engaging in the dialogue is the failure to include Latin American/Peruvian regional travel writers. Though some scholars include in their studies a look at Latin American voices or texts of resistance to the representations written about Latin American countries, I was struck by their tendency to look for those voices and texts of protest outside of the travel-writing genre itself. For example, Pratt looks to Latin American nineteenth-century essayists and poets – with the exception of Sarmiento's travel texts and *Facundo*. Poole focuses on Peruvian photographers such as Martín Chambi. She does examine Fuentes' work but concentrates most of her analysis on his illustrations. Wilson foregoes the travel-writing genre altogether and turns his focus, instead, toward early twentieth-century and contemporary Latin American fiction; and Catlin examines Latin American painters and illustrators of the mid-1800s. This gap allows for researchers like Wilson to make the following conclusion:

> There is not a strong tradition of Latin American empirical observation or of Latin American travel writing, and even less on travelling within the Latin American continent. Sarmiento is a good example of a writer capable of creating a hybrid text based on travel literature…but his actual travel writing only explored the United States and Europe. (Wilson 803)

In light of the current scholarship regarding the topic of nineteenth-century travel narratives regarding Peru specifically, two questions in particular came to mind for me. First, did Latin Americans—and more specifically, Peruvians—produce any regional travelogues about their own countries during the same period that imperialist travelers were authorizing themselves to represent Peru and Peruvian culture? If such travelogues existed, did European and North American travelers ever cite those travel texts or other Peruvian-authored predecessor texts, which could suggest that the dialogue concerning Peru's then-current state and future was bidirectional? The results of this book answers both those initial questions affirmatively as demonstrated and discussed in the chapters, Ghosts in the Machine and Talking Back to Center(s). Peruvians such as Bustamante, Fuentes, and Valdéz y Palacios were writing texts which allowed them to proffer representations of their own country precisely to refute those representations of Peru published by foreign travel writers. And, in the cases of Fuentes and Bustamante, not only were they engaging in the dialogue, but also were, indeed, cited by travelers such as von Tschudi, Scherzer and Squier. This opens up an additional terrain for post-colonialists to examine in an effort to dispell the notion of the "master subject." How masterful can such a subject be if s/he is compelled to incorporate the publications written by the intellectuals in the other land?

Talking Back to Center(s) also examined how Peruvian writers, in their push to authorize themselves (and in their allegiences to their own versions of what constitutes Peruvian national culture) engage in tropes of othering. In the contest to attempt the construction of a national imaginary, serrano nationalists and limeño nationalsits were talking back to one another's nationalist agendas as well as talking back to the denigrating representations of Peruvian culture they found in imperialist travel writing about their country.

In all of the chapters, attention was paid to the explicitly dialogic nature of travel writing concerning nineteenth-century Peru; how each type of writer taking on the topic of Peru engaged in constructing hierarchies of superiority due to their agendas' discursive need for the Other; and how each participant involved was in a constant state of multiple subjectivities due to trying to maintain his/her authority as a writing subject.

Suggestions for furthering the field
Upon trying to find regional travel texts produced by Peruvian writers during the nineteenth-century, I was able to unearth several travel writings - by non-Peruvian and Peruvian writers alike—which either have received little attention or none at all by postcolonialists in the field. Some of these texts were considered either empirically authoritative (such as those by von Tschudi, Scherzer and Fuentes) or were popular favorites (such as those produced by Dahlgren and Carleton). Other travel writers such as Pfieffer, Bustamante and Dahlgren have been included in studies but not in reference to their works concerning Peru. Still others have yet to receive attention as in the cases of Valdéz y Palacios, Scherzer, De Sartiges, von Tschudi and Vincent.

Before conclusions can be made such as Wilson's that "there is not a strong tradition of Latin American...travel writing," I suggest further research needs to take place among specialists in the field to find additional examples of Latin American regional travel texts on a country to country basis. If I found examples such as those written by Bustamante and Valdez y Palacios, I propose there are others yet to be uncovered. Beyond archival research to find such texts, close attention given to the citational practices of imperialist travel writers is a valuable resource to find regional travelogues. Their proclivity to cite other travel texts includes often footnoting works written by Latin

Americans. Such was the case with the works of Bustamante and Fuentes. Since Catlin and Poole have found costumbrismo's influence on the genre, the study of Latin American costumbrista texts will likely add to a more thorough consideration of nineteenth-century Latin American voices. Additionally, a look into periodicals might prove useful, since writers such as Fuentes, Brand, Squire, and Dahlgren allude to travel writers who published extracts of their travel stories in newspapers.

Finally, I suggest that a way to decenter the Eurocentric notion of what constitutes Travel (with a capital T) in the first place and how that notion mutes Latin American travelogues written about Latin America itself. Have some researchers been suaded by Columbus' departure and arrival points and his *Diario* as the "originary moment" with which to define Travel, thereby overlooking the existence of Latin American regional travel writing (Loomba 108)? If the Western monomythic form of travel and story requires that the heroic traveler achieve a "passage beyond the Known into the unknown," as Joseph Campbell suggests, are we not limiting our view of the genre itself and the multiple participants who engage in it (82)?

A turn toward unearthing Latin American regional travelogues would serve to broaden our definitions of both travel and the "travel adventurer" who attempts it, thereby allowing in the republican travel-adventurer who contests imperialist representations and exposes regions of his or her own country.

Bibliography

Core travelogues:

Bustamante, Juan. *Viaje al Antiguo Mundo.* 1849. Lima: Primer Festival del Libro Puneño, 1959.
Fuentes, Manuel A. *Lima: Apuntes históricos, descriptivos, estadísticos y de costumbres.* 1867. Lima: Fondo
   del Libro Banco Industrial del Perú, 1985.
Dahlgren, Madeleine Vinton. *South Sea Sketches: A Narrative.* Boston: James R. Osgood and Co., 1881.
Tristan, Flora. *Peregrinaciones de una paria.* 1838. Ed. and trans. Emilia Romero. Lima: Editorial Cul-tural Antártica S.A., 1946.
Tschudi, J.J. von. *Travels in Peru, during the Years 1838-1842.* 1847. Trans. Thomasina Ross. New York: Wiley and Putnam, 1847.
Valdéz y Palacios, J.M. *Viaje del Cuzco a Belen en el Gran Para.* 1844. Ed. Estuardo Núñez. Lima: Biblioteca Nacional del Perú, 1971.

Additional travelogues:

Brand, Charles. *Journal of Voyage to Peru.* 1828. London: Henry Colburn, 1828.
Carleton, George. *Our Artist in Peru.* 1866. New York: Harpers and Bros., 1866.
Cólon, Cristóbal. *Diario de abordo.* 1492-1493. Ed. Luis Arranz. Madrid: Historia 16, 1985.
Darwin, Charles. *The Voyage of the Beagle.* 1839. Washington, D.C.: National Geographic Classics, 2004.
De Sartiges, E. "Viaje a las repúblicas de América del Sur." 1834. *Dos viajeros franceses en el Perú Repblicano.* Trans. Emilia Romero. Lima: Editorial Cultura Antártica, S.A., 1947.
Humboldt, Alexander von. "Diario del Perú." Trans. Manuel Vegas Vélez. *Humboldt en el Perú.* Piura, Perú: CIPCA, 1991.
Lastarria, José Victoriano. "Lima en 1850." *Viajeros en el Perú Republicano.* Ed. George Schade. Lima: Universidad Nacional Mayor de San Marcos, 1971.
Markham, Clements R. *Cuzco and Lima.* London: Chapman and Hall, 1856.
Pfeiffer, Ida. *A Lady's Second Journey around the World.* New York: Harper and Bros., 1856.
Rivero, Mariano Eudardo de and J.J. von Tschudi. *Antiguedades peruanas.* Arequipa: Primer Festival del Libro Arequipeño, 1958.
Squier, E.G. *Peru: Incidents of Travel and Exploration in the Land of the Incas.* 1877. New York: AMS P, 1973.
Scherzer, Karl. *Visita al Perú en 1859.* Ed. and trans. Estuardo Nuñez. Lima: Universidad Nacional Mayor de San Marcos, 1971.
Vincent, E. Howard. *China to Peru: Over the Andes.* London: Sampson Low, Marston & Co., 1894.

Secondary sources:

Agosín, Marjorie and Julie Levison, eds. *Magical Sites: Women Travelers in Nineteenth-Century Latin America.* Buffalo, New York: White Pine P, 1999.
Allen, Esther. "This Is Not America: Nineteenth-century Accounts of Travel between the Americas." Diss. New York U, 1992.
Ayala, José Valdizán. "El Perú: 1821-1879." *Hisotiria del Perú republicano.* Ed. José Valdizán Ayala, Lima: Fondo de Desarrollo Editorial, 1997.

Bann, Stephen. "Travelling to Collect: The Booty of John Bargrave and Charles Waterton." *Travellers' Tales: Narratives of Home and Displacement.* Ed. George Robertson, Melinda Mash, Lisa Tickner, Jon Bird, Barry Curtis and Tim Putnam. New York: Routledge, 1994. 155-163.

Barnhart, Robert. ed. *Chambers Dictionary of Etymology.* New York: Chambers, 2001.

Barrera-Osorio, Antonio. *Experiencing Nature: The Spanish American Empire and the Early Scientific Revolution.* Austin: U of Texas P, 2006.

Bell, Duncan. "From Ancient to Modern in Victorian Imperial Thought." *The Historical Journal* 49.3 (2006): 1-25.

Betancourt, J.V. "Los curros del manglar." *Costumbristas cubanos del siglo XX.* Ed. Salvador Bueno. Caracas: Ayacucho, 1985.

Blake, Susan. "A Woman's Trek: What Difference Does Gender Make." *Women and Imperialism.* Ed. Nupur Chaudhuri and Margaret Strobel. Bloomington: Indiana UP, 1992. 19-34.

Blunt, Alison. *Travel, Gender, and Imperialism: Mary Kingsley and West Africa.* New York: The Guilford P, 1994.

Blunt, Alison and Gillian Rose. *Writing Women and Space: Colonial and Postcolonial Geographies.* New York: Guilford P, 1994.

Bonilla, Heraclio. "Peru and Bolivia." *Spanish America after Independence, c. 1820-c.1870.* Ed. Leslie Bethel. Cambridge: Cambridge UP, 1987.

Brushwood, John. *Genteel Barbarism: New Readings of Nineteenth-Century Spanish American Novels.* Lincoln: U of Nebraska P, 1981.

Bueno, Salvador. Prólogo. *Costumbristas cubanos del siglo XX.* Ed. Salvador Bueno. Caracas: Ayacucho, 1985.

Bulmer-Thomas, Victore, John Coatsworth and Roberto Cortes-Conde, ed. *The Cambridge Economic History of Latin America: Volume 1, The Colonial Era and the Short Nineteenth Century.* New York: Cambridge UP, 2005.

Burke, Janet and Ted Humphrey. *Ninetennth-Century Nation Building and the Latin American Intellectual Tradition.* Indianapolis: Hackett Publishing Co., 2007.

Burton, Antoinette. "The White Woman's Burden: British Feminists and 'The Indian Woman,' 1865-1915." *Women and Imperialism.* Ed. Nupur Chaudhuri and Margaret Strobel. Bloomington: Indiana UP, 1992. 137-157.

Bushnell, David and Neill Macaulay. *The Emergence of Latin America in the Nineteenth Century.* 2nd edition. New York: Oxford UP, 1994.

Cahill, David. *Crown, From Rebellion to Independence in the Andes: Soundings from Southern Peru, 1750-1830.* Amsterdam: Asksant Academic Publishers, 2002.

Cahill, David and Blanca Tovias, ed. *New World, First Nations: Native Peoples of Mesoamerica and the Andes Under Colonial Rule.* Sussex: Sussex Academic P, 2006.

Callaway, Helen and Dorothy Helly. "Crusader for Empire: Flora Shaw/Lady Lugard." *Women and Imperialism.* Ed. Nupur Chaudhuri and Margaret Strobel. Bloomington: Indiana UP, 1992. 79-97.

Campbell, Joseph. *The Hero with a Thousand Faces.* Princeton: Princeton UP, 1973.

Campbell, Mary. *The Witness and the Other World: Exotic European Travel Writing.* Ithaca: Cornell UP, 1988.

Cañizares-Esguerra, Jorge. *Nature, Empire, and Nation: Explorations of the History of Science in the Iberian World.* Stanford: Stanford UP, 2006.

——. "Postcolonialsm avant la lettre: Travelers and Clerics inEighteenth-Century Colonial Spanish America." *After Spanish Rule.* Ed. Andrés Guerrero and Mark Thurner. Durham: Duke UP, 2003.

Castro-Klarén and John Charles Chasteen, ed. *Beyond Imagined Communities: Reading and Writing the Nation in Nineteenth-Century Latin America*. Baltimore: Johns Hopkins UP, 2003.

Catlin, Stanton. "Traveller-Reporter Artists and the Empirical Tradition in Post-Independence Latin American Art." *Art in Latin America: The Modern Era, 1820-1890*. Ed. Dawn Ades. New Haven, CT: Yale UP, 1989.

Chang-Rodríguez, Raquel and Malva E. Filer. *Voces de Hispanoamérica: Antología literaria*. Boston: Thomson-Heinle, 2004.

Clayton, Lawrence. "Peru: Dominance of Private Businessmen." *United States and Latin American Relations, 1850-1903*. Ed. Thomas Leonard. Tuscaloosa, Alabama: The U of Alabama P, 1991.

Cornejo Polar, Jorge. "Relaciones entre el costumbrismo peruano y el español." *Cuadernos Hispanoamericanos* 539 (1995): 59-77.

Coronil, Fernando. Foreword. *Close Encounters of Empire*. Joseph Gilbert, Ed. Catherine LeGrand and Ricardo Salvatore. Durham: Duke UP, 1998. 162-189.

Cross, Maire. *The Letter in Flora Tristan's Politics, 1835-1844*. Hampshire: Palgrave Macmillan, 2004.

Curtis, Barry and Claire Pajaczkowska. "Getting There: Travel, Time and Narrative." *Travellers' Tales: Narratives of Home and Displacement*. Ed. George Robertson, Melinda Mash, Lisa Tickner, Jon Bird, Barry Curtis and Tim Putnam. New York: Routledge, 1994. 199-215.

Fitzell, Jill. "Cultural Colonialism and Ethnography: European Travellers in Nineteenth Century Ecuador." Diss. U of British Columbia. 1994.

Fombona Iribarren, Jacinto Rafael. "El texto de viajes de la época modernista. Viajeros hispanoamericanos y la construcción de Europa." Diss. Yale U. 1993.

Franco, Jean. *An Introduction to Spanish-American Literature*. NY: Cambridge UP, 1994.

Fussell, Paul. *The Norton Book of Travel*. New York: W.W. Norton & Co., 1987.

Garcilaso de la Vega, Inca. *Comentarios reales*. 1609. Ed. Aurelio Miro Quesada. Caracas: Biblioteca Ayacucho, 1991.

Garrett, David. *Shadows of Empire: The Indian Nobility of Cuzco, 1750-1825*. New York: Cambirdge UP, 2005.

Geertz, Clifford. *Interpretation of Cultures*. New York: Basic Books, Inc., Publishers, 1973.

Gerbi, Antonello. *The Dispute of the New World*. Trans. Jeremy Moyle. Pittsburgh: U of Pittsburgh P, 1973.

Gootenberg, Paul. *Between Silver and Guano: Commercial Policy and the State in Postindependence Peru*. Princeton: Princeton UP, 1989.

Greenblatt, Stephen. *Marvelous Possessions: The Wonder of the New World*. Chicago: U of Chicago P, 1991.

Hahner, June. *Women through Women's Eyes: Latin American Women in Nineteenth-Century Travel Accounts*. Wilmington: SR Books, 1998.

Hart, Kathleen. "An I for and Eye: Flora Tristan and Female Visual Allegory." *Nineteenth-Century French Studies* 26.1 (1997): 52-65.

Jacobsen, Nils. *Mirages of Transition: The Peruvian Altiplano, 1780-1930*. Berkeley: U of California P, 1993.

Jacobsen, Nils and Cristóbal Aljovín de Losada, ed. *Political Cultures in the Andes, 1750-1950*. Durham: Duke UP, 2005.

Jara, René and Nicholas Spadaccini. Introduction. *Amerindian Images and the Legacy of Columbus*. Ed. René Jara and Nicholas Spadaccini. Minneapolis: U of Minnesota P, 1992.

Larson, Brooke. *Trials of Nation Making: Liberalism, Race, and Ethnicity in the Andes, 1810-1910*. New York: Cambridge UP, 2004.

Las Casas, Bartolomé de. *Brevísima relación de la destrucción de Las Indias*. 1552. Ed. Consuelo Varela. Madrid: Castalia, 1999.
Leed, Eric. *The Mind of the Traveler: From Gilgamesh to Global Tourism*. New York: Basic Books, 1991.
Loomba, Ania. *Colonialism/Postcolonialism*. London: Routledge, 1998.
MacCormack, Sabine. *On the Wings of Time: Rome, the Incas, Spain, and Peru*. Princeton: Princeton UP, 2006.
Marmontel, Jean François. *Les Incas*. 1770. Paris: n.p., 1777.
Metwalli, A.M. "Americans Abroad: The Popular Art of Travel Writing in the Nineteenth Century." *Exploration* 4.1 (1976): 15-24.
Mills, Sara. *Discourses of Difference: An Analysis of Women's Travel Writing and Colonialism*. New York: Routledge, 1991.
Morris, Mary, ed. *Maiden Voyages: Writings of Women Travelers*. New York: Vintage Books, 1993.
Morris, Pam. Introduction. *The Bakhtin Reader: Selected Writings of Bakhtin, Medvedev, Voloshinov*. Ed. Pam Morris. London: Edward Arnold, 1994.
Muecke, Ulrich. *Political Culture in Nineteenth-Century Peru: The Rise of the Partido Civil*. Pittsburg: U of Pittsburgh P, 2004.
Niles, Blair. *Peruvian Pageant: A Journey in Time*. Indianapolis: The Bobbs-Merrill Co., 1937.
Nuñez, Estuardo. *Viajeros alemanes al Perú*. Lima: Universidad Nacional Mayor de San Marcus, 1971.
———. *Viajeros hispanoamericanos (Temas continentales)*. Caracas: Bibiloteca Ayacucho, 1989.
Paz Soldán, Mariano Felipe. *Historia del Perú independiente: Primer Período, 1819-1822*. Havre: Imprenta de Alfonso LEMALE, 1868.
Pollock, Griselda. "Territories of Desire: Reconsiderations of an African Childhood." *Travellers' Tales: Narratives of Home and Displacement*. Ed. George Robertson, Melinda Mash, Lisa Tickner, Jon Bird, Barry Curtis and Tim Putnam. New York: Routledge, 1994. 63-92.
Poole, Deborah. "Landscape and the Imperial Subject." *Close Encounters of Empire*. Ed. Joseph Gilbert, Catherine LeGrand and Ricardo Salvatore. Durham: Duke UP, 1998. 162-189.
———. "One-Eyed Gaze: Gender in Nineteenth Century Illustrations of Peru." *Dialectical Anthropology* 13 (1988): 333-364.
———. *Vision, Race, and Modernity: A Visual Economy of the Andean Image World*. Princeton, NJ: Princeton UP, 1997.
Porter, Dennis. *Haunted Journeys: Desire and Transgression in European Travel Writing*. Princeton: Princeton UP, 1991.
Preminger, Alex and T.V.F. Brogan, ed. *The New Princeton Encyclopedia of Poetry and Poetics*. New York: MJF Books, 1993.
Premo, Bianca. *Children of the Father King: Youth, Authority and Legal Minority in Colonial Lima*. Chapel Hill: U of North Carolina P, 2006.
Prescott, William H. *History of the Conquest of Peru*. 1868. New York: American Publishers Corporation, n.d.
Pupo-Walker, Enrique. "Reflexiones para otras lecturas del relato costumbrista." *Revista de Estudios Hispánicos* 24.2 (1990): 13-37.
Ramos, Julio. *Divergent Modernities: Culture and Politics in Nineteenth-Century Latin America*. Trans. John D. Blanco. Durham: Duke UP, 2001.
Ramusak, Barbara. "Cultural Missionaries, Maternal Imperialists, Feminist Allies: British Women Activists in India, 1865-1945." *Women and Imperialism*. Ed. Nupur Chaudhuri and Margaret Strobels. Bloomington: Indiana UP, 1992. 119-136.

Ranciere, Jacques. "Discovering New Worlds: Politics of Travel and Metaphors of Space." *Travellers' Tales: Narratives of Home and Displacement*. Ed. George Robertson, Melinda Mash, Lisa Tickner, Jon Bird, Barry Curtis and Tim Putnam. New York: Routledge, 1994. 29-37.

Robertson, William. *The History of America*. 2 vols. London: W. Strahan, 1777-78.

Sachs, Aaron. *The Humboldt Current: Nineteenth-Century Exploration and the Roots of American Environmentalism*. New York: Viking Adult, 2006.

Salvatore, Ricardo. "North American Travel Narratives and the Ordering/Othering of South America." *Journal of Historical Sociology* 9.1 (1996): 85-110.

Sarup, Madan. "Home and Identity." Travellers' Tales: Narratives of Home and Displacement. Ed. George Robertson, Melinda Mash, Lisa Tickner, Jon Bird, Barry Curtis and Tim Putnam. New York: Routledge, 1994. 93-104.

Schriber, Mary. *Writing Home: American Women Abroad, 1830-1920*. Charlottesville: UP of Virgina, 1997.

Schwartz, Stuart. "Colonial Identities and the Sociedad de Castas." *Colonial Latin American Review* 4.1 (1995): 185-201.

Skidmore, Thomas S. and Peter H. Smih. *Modern Latin America*. New York: Oxford UP, 1997.

Smith, Sidonie and Julia Watson. *Women, Autobiography, Theory: A Reader*. Madison: U of Wisconsin P, 1998.

Strobel, Margaret. *European Women and the Second British Empire*. Bloomington: Indiana UP, 1991.

Suzarte, José Quintín. "Los guajiros." *Costumbristas cubanos del siglo XX*. Ed. Salvador Bueno. Caracas: Ayacucho, 1985.

Szurmuk, Mónica. "'Viajeras': Women's Travel Writing and the Construction of Self and National Identity in Argentina, 1850-1930." Diss. U of California, San Diego. 1994.

Tenorio Trillo, Mauricio. "Essaying the History of National Images." *After Spanish Rule*. Ed. Andrés Guerrero and Mark Thurner. Durham: Duke UP, 2003.

Terdiman, Richard. *Discourse/Counter-Discourse: The Theory and Practice of Symbolic Resistance in Nineteenth-Century France*. Ithaca: Cornell UP, 1985.

Thurner, Mark. *From Two Republics to One Divided: Contradictions of Postcolonial Nationmaking in Andean Peru*. Durham: Duke UP, 1997.

———. "Peruvian Genealogies of History and Nation." *After Spanish Rule*. Ed. Andrés Guerrero and Mark Thurner. Durham: Duke UP, 2003.

Tinling, Marion. *With Women's Eyes: Visitors to the New World, 1775-1918*. Hamden, Connecticut: Archon Books, 1993.

Trigo, Benigno. *Subjects of Crisis: Race and Gender as Disease in Latin America*. Hanover: Wesleyan UP, 2000.

Unanue, José Hipolito. *Nuevo día del Perú*. Trujillo: n.p., 1824.

———. *Observaciones sobre el clima de Lima*. Madrid: Sancha, 1815.

Verdevoye, Paul. "Costumbrismo y americanismo en la obra de Domingo Faustino Sarmiento." *Sur* 351 (1977): 55-70.

Viñas, David. *Literatura argentina y realidad política: De Sarmiento a Cortázar*. Buenos Aires: Ediciones Siglo Veinte, 1971.

Walker, Charles. *Smoldering Ashes: Cuzco and the Creation of Republican Peru, 1780-1840*. Durham: Duke UP, 1999.

Ware, Vron. *Beyond the Pale: White Women, Racism and History*. London: Verso, 1992.

Wertheimer, Eric. *Imagined Empires: Incas, Aztecs, and the New World of American Literature, 1771-1876*. Cambridge: Cambridge UP, 1999.

Wilson, Jason. "Travel Literature." *Encyclopedia of Latin American Literature*. Ed. Verity Smith. London: FD, 1997.
Zamora, Margarita. *Reading Columbus*. Berkeley: U of California P, 1993.

Theoretical and methodological framework:
Anderson, Benedict. *Imagined Communities*. London: Verso, 1991.
Ashcroft, Bill, Gareth Griffiths and Helen Tiffin, ed. *The Post-Colonial Studies Reader*. New York: Routledge, 1995.
Bakhtin, M.M. *The Dialogic Imagination: Four Essays*. Ed. Michael Holquist. Trans. Michael Holquist and Caryl Emerson. Austin: U of Texas P, 1981.
——. "Language as Dialogic Interation." *The Bakhtin Reader: Selected Writings of Bakhtin, Medvedev, Voloshinov*. Ed. Pam Morris. London: Edward Arnold, 1994. 48-61.
——. *Marxism and the Philosophy of Language*. Trans. L. Matejka and I. R. Titunik. Cambridge: Harvard UP, 1973.
Bhabha, Homi. "DissemiNation: time, narrative, and the margins of the modern nation." *Nation and Narration*. Ed. Homi Bhabha. New York: Routledge, 1990.
——. *The Location of Culture*. New York: Routledge, 1994.
——. "Postcolonial Criticism." *Redrawing the Boundaries: The Transformation of English and American Literary Studies*. Ed. Stephen Greenblatt and Giles Gunn. New York: The Modern Language Association of America, 1992.
Butler, Judith. *Bodies that Matter*. New York: Routledge, 1993.
——. *Gender Trouble: Feminism and the Subversion of Identity*. New York: Routledge, 1990.
Chatterjee, Partha. *Nationalist Thought and the Colonial World: A Derivative Discourse*. Avon: Zed Books, Ltd., 1986.
Fabian, Johannes. *Time and the Other: How Anthropology Makes Its Object*. New York: Columbia UP, 1983.
Foucault, Michel. *The Archaeology of Knowledge*. Trans. A.M.S. Smith. New York: Pantheon, 1972.
——. *The History of Sexuality*. Trans. Robert Hurley. New York: Vintage Books, 1980.
Mignolo, Walter. *The Darker Side of the Renaissance: Literacy, Territoriality, and Colonization*. Ann Arbor: The U of Michigan P, 1995.
——. "Editor's Introduction." *Poetics Today* 15.4 (1994): 505-521.
Minh-ha, Trinh. *Woman, Native, Other*. Bloomington: U of Indiana P, 1989.
Pile, Steve and Nigel Thrift. *Mapping the Subject: Geographies of Cultural Transformation*. New York: Routledge,1995.
Pratt, Mary Louise. *Imperial Eyes: Travel Writing and Transculturation*. New York: Routledge, 1992.
Spurr, David. *The Rhetoric of Empire: Colonial Discourse in Journalism, Travel Writing and Imperial Administration*. Durham: Duke UP, 1992.
White, Hayden. *The Content of the Form: Narrative Discourse and Historical Representation*. Baltimore: Johns Hopkins UP, 1987.
——. *Tropics of Discourse: Essays in Cultural Criticism*. Baltimore: Johns Hopkins UP, 1978.

Currents in Comparative
Romance Languages and Literatures

This series was founded in 1987, and actively solicits book-length manuscripts (approximately 200–400 pages) that treat aspects of Romance languages and literatures. Originally established for works dealing with two or more Romance literatures, the series has broadened its horizons and now includes studies on themes within a single literature or between different literatures, civilizations, art, music, film and social movements, as well as comparative linguistics. Studies on individual writers with an influence on other literatures/civilizations are also welcome. We entertain a variety of approaches and formats, provided the scholarship and methodology are appropriate.

For additional information about the series or for the submission of manuscripts, please contact:

> Tamara Alvarez-Detrell and Michael G. Paulson
> c/o Dr. Heidi Burns
> Peter Lang Publishing, Inc.
> P.O. Box 1246
> Bel Air, MD 21014-1246

To order other books in this series, please contact our Customer Service Department:

> 800-770-LANG (within the U.S.)
> 212-647-7706 (outside the U.S.)
> 212-647-7707 FAX

or browse online by series at:

> www.peterlang.com